Enjoy Nigeria
(A Travel Guide)

Ian Nason

Spectrum Books Limited
Ibadan • Owerri • Kaduna • Lagos

Published by
Spectrum Books Limited
Sunshine House
1 Emmanuel Alayande Street
Oluyole Estate
Ibadan, Nigeria

in association with
Safari Books (Export) Limited
Bell Royal House
Hilgrove Street
St Helier, Jersey
Channel Island, UK

© Ian Nason 1991

All rights reserved. This book is copyright and so no part of it may be reproduced, stored in a retrieval system or transmitted in any form or by any means, electronic, mechanical, electrostatic, magnetic tape, photocopying, recording, or otherwise without the express permission of the author who is the copyright owner.

First published 1991
Revised Edition 1993

ISBN 978 246 225 X

Printed by Intec Printers Limited, Ibadan

Dedication

I dedicate this book to my two grandsons and to the people of Bakana Island, Rivers State, who conferred on me the honorary chieftaincy title of Aku Tubo of Bakana in March, 1990. Also to the Nigerian Conservation Foundation whose efforts to protect the flora and fauna of Nigeria for its future generations deserve every encouragement. To all these recipients I donate the royalties from the sale of this book.

Contents

	Acknowledgements	vi
	Foreword	viii
	Introduction	ix
1.	**Lagos**	1
2.	**South-west** The area south-west of the River Niger	10
3.	**South-east** The area south-east of the Niger and Benue Rivers	49
4.	**North-west** The area north of the River Niger which includes the states of Niger, Sokoto, Kaduna, Kano, Katsina, Kebbi and the Federal Capital Territory	76
5.	**North-east** The area north of the River Benue including the states of Borno, Yobe, Jigawa, Bauchi, Plateau and parts of Benue, Taraba and Adamawa	106

Acknowledgements

Firstly, I must thank my dear wife, who has been my companion on many of my travels, for patiently typing, correcting, proof reading and bearing with me over this whole project, which has been far more demanding than I had ever imagined. I must also thank those who have sent me reports of tourist sites and directed me to them. Amongst these are Tasso Leventis of the Leventis Group; Les Hodgson, the former Manager of African Timber and Plywood at Sapele, Paul Williams and George Edgar, both of the British High Commission, Lagos, who are intrepid travellers and have charted new routes for others to follow.

I have received advice, encouragement and sound criticism from many others which has forced me to re-check my information and redouble my efforts towards finding suitable tourist sites, not only for the international community, but also for the domestic market, as without a sound domestic market demanding high standards, tourism will fail to realise its full potential in Nigeria. For this advice, I owe a debt to Colonel Tony Ukpo, Principal Staff Officer to the President; Hajia Zainab Duke, an author who suggested the more positive title of *Enjoy Nigeria*, and Tom Harris of the British High Commission who has my doubtful gratitude for suggesting that I write a travel brief in the first place!

Further thanks must go to all those who helped to sell my original three travel booklets called *Travel Nigeria*. Without their help I would never have attempted this book. Although I am unable to mention the names of everybody who contributed in the preparation of this book, I would particularly like to pay tribute to Fons and Leny Claessen, the joint Secretaries of the Nigerian Field

Society (NFS); Ros Pearce, of NFS; Sandra Forsyth of the British Wives Group; John Pease of Schlumberger, Port Harcourt; Lt Colonel Albert Beraud from France and Brigadier Habib from Egypt and other fellow Defence Advisers who checked the manuscript, and Freddie Scott of the West Africa Committee, who was responsible for putting me in touch with Spectrum Books and many of the advertisers.

Finally, I must thank my sponsors who have kindly advertised in this book. Without their help the book could not have 'taken off'. I hope the success of the book will reward them for their backing.

No book can reach the market place without a good publisher. Joop Berkhout and Spectrum Books receive my admiration for running the usual commercial risks by accepting *Enjoy Nigeria*.

I apologise if I have left anyone out, but to everyone else who has helped I send my grateful thanks.

State House
Lagos
Nigeria

15th June, 1990

Chief Colonel I.G. Nason, OSC (Nig) N.D.C., p.sc
Defence Adviser
British High Commission
LAGOS

Dear Ian,

1. I was delighted to have my attention drawn to your work titled: "Enjoy Nigeria".

2. At a time when we are hoping to promote our tourist industry in order to boost foreign exchange earnings, at a time when Nigerians and the world at large are becoming increasingly aware of the scenic beauty and the cultural riches of this nation, I consider your work both timely and apt.

3. It is my hope, however, that in view of the dynamic nature of progress, this fascinating piece of work will be periodically up-dated, to encapsulate new developments.

4. I commend your efforts and wish you every success.

Yours Sincerely

Ibrahim B’gida

General Ibrahim B Babangida
President
Commander-In-Chief
Armed Forces of Nigeria

viii

Introduction

General

In 1979, when I first came to Nigeria, I found that many people had a wealth of travel information in their heads but had put little down on paper. I therefore produced 'A Newcomer's Guide to Kaduna', with a request at the end asking readers to write up their travel experiences and include the notes in the back of the guide. This my contemporaries in Kaduna did most enthusiastically, and on returning to Nigeria in 1987, I was delighted to see that the idea had been expanded and a booklet called, 'The British Advisory Team Travel Notes' was in circulation. It is now time to expand again and also to update some of the information, which is constantly changing as Nigeria develops new roads, hotels and tourist assets.

My thanks must go to the many people who have written up their own trips in order that others can avoid some of the pitfalls of travel in Nigeria. The pioneer traveller in Nigeria has a difficult time even after taking advice. Only major roads are signed, (although this situation is improving), maps are often inaccurate, the wet season rains or dry season harmattan can blemish a journey and the numerous police, customs, immigration and local government road blocks all add to the difficulties and delays encountered. Add to those, the occasional enormous car-damaging potholes and eroded roadsides, the risk of accident and the unpredictable taxi driver ('Let Them Say!'), who would dare to venture outside the relative security of his own home? The fact that we do is because there is so much to see and do in Nigeria. It is my intention to show you how much you are missing if you do not travel in and around Nigeria. It is a fascinating country with a vast range of landscapes from the mangrove swamps of the delta area to the semi-arid Sahel region of the north, with a corresponding change in the life-styles of the people.

Scope

To keep these notes simple there is little information on the geography, history, climate or culture of Nigeria, but there are many books covering these matters, e.g *Nigeria, Giant of Africa,* by Peter Holmes, *The Living Arts of Nigeria,* by William Fagg, *Nigeria,* by Jaqueline Redith; *Nigeria, The Land, its Art and its People — an Anthology* by Frederick Lumley; and *Nigeria, the Land and its People* by Richard Synge. These books can fill some of the gaps in our knowledge, and if they are not available in bookshops, they may be found in libraries such as the British Council Library in Kingsway Road, Lagos.

I have divided Nigeria into 4 regions rather than covering each state separately, to make it easier for the traveller. The regions will be further divided into areas around main towns as these towns usually have the best hotels. The towns are listed in alphabetical order. Most of the journeys will be based on travel from Lagos.

A simple guidebook like this cannot possibly cover all the tourist spots, roads, accommodation and distances. I apologise in advance for any mistakes in detail, routes, etc., because it would be impossible to keep it completely up-to-date. Nevertheless, the information is the best available at the time of writing. I have not included many maps, because if maps cannot show all the details they tend to confuse rather than help. I have found during my years in Nigeria that, with few exceptions, if you ask the local people you will get the right answer and they often go out of their way to help, even to the extent of offering to guide you themselves.

Information

There are a number of vital pieces of information that everyone wants to know when travelling, so the following will be included: roads, routes, timings, accommodation, the tourist site itself, and miscellaneous information. Costs are not included because they change so often and can confuse the tourist. Take up-to-date advice.

Preparation

It is worth carrying out some form of preparation before travelling. Time must be made to check on spare tyres, tyre pump, jack, spares like fan belts, etc., petrol cans for some more remote parts of Nigeria, or when there is a temporary distribution problem. Remember that water is vital in the tropics. You may feel comfortable in your air-conditioned car when all is well, but what happens if it breaks down and you are kilometers away from any village, wrestling with a puncture in the mid-day sun? Always plan on the worst case, especially with children. When you are travelling with children remember to take some car games and books. However, do not overload your car; you will probably regret it when your car meets a large pothole! It is advisable to take emergency telephone numbers with you, and leave a copy of your route with a friend.

Documentation

It is wise to carry the following documents:
    a.   Valid driving licence (Nigerian).
    b.   Driving licence from your country of origin, for expatriates.
    c.   Passport or identity card for hotels

d. Third party insurance.
   e. Car registration document.

Fuel, Water and Medicine

Fuel is usually readily available in Nigeria, except in the more remote areas, but occasionally there are local shortages particularly at Christmas time, or when a refinery is temporarily out of action, so it is sometimes necessary to take jerrycans.

Water is essential if you are camping. If you are staying in hotels it is still useful to have some bottled water, or you can order it from the hotel, as the water in plastic bottles in hotel fridges is usually tap water. Never be without water on a journey in case of a puncture or breakdown when you might have to exert yourself in the heat. Lack of water and salt can lead to dehydration, with resulting headaches, cramp and in a bad case, heat exhaustion, which needs medical attention. Salt is vital in the tropics when you are sweating a great deal.

A first-aid kit is essential for cuts, stings, stomach illnesses, headaches and sunburn. A lotion for dry skin is useful in the north during the dry season when skin can become as parched as the landscape. With the risk of AIDS, it is worth taking a kit for blood transfusions in case of accident. Take your own anti-malarial prophylactics and any drugs and pills you might need as medicines are not always available locally.

Up-to-date Information

It is commonsense, but it is worth mentioning — do ask around your friends and contacts before setting out on a major expedition, just to check on the essentials. Roads may have either improved or deteriorated.

The People

In my experience, the people in Nigeria are incredibly friendly and cheerful. They love a laugh and have a great sense of fun. They are always willing to help, sometimes at great inconvenience to themselves, so do not be afraid to ask. Remember that in a hot climate tempers can fray very quickly, but a joke can often dissipate a potentially difficult situation. Nigerians love giving and receiving gifts, so be prepared by taking gifts with you, particularly something from your own country.

If you have received assistance you will be expected to pay some 'dash', but if a large service is involved, e.g. pushing your car out of the mud, negotiate with the village headman or the people concerned beforehand to prevent arguments later. Do not be pushy when you go into a village or sacred area. Always take the advice of the village headman or spokesman. There are certain things you are not allowed to see or photograph. Do not insist or sneak a photograph, as this could cause serious offence. Be careful about photography. In general, ask before photographing people, especially women. Do not photograph government buildings, military installations or border areas. Binoculars can be mistaken for a camera, so bird-watchers, beware! Finally, when seeking information, always exchange greetings before asking directly for assistance, as this is the Nigerian custom.

Summary

In order to enjoy a trouble-free journey in Nigeria, it is essential to plan and prepare. You will never regret finding the time to prepare your car and collect the essentials: food, water, maps, documents and especially medical requirements. For those who are used to travelling in Europe and America, there are a number of differences to travelling in West Africa. You are travelling in an area where not all the roads are signed, where communication is sparse and accommodation is not always up to the standard of the international traveller. If you do get into difficulties, there are few breakdown trucks, few road patrolmen, no ambulances on alert and few well-equipped garages. I emphasise that this is not a criticism of Nigeria, but 'Rome was not built in a day'. Nigeria is still developing and full facilities are not yet available for the tourist. The answer is:

a. Drive carefully and defensively, beware of the unpredictable and it is advisable not to drive at night.
b. Take all you need for yourself and passengers, especially children.
c. Take all you need for your car.
d. Have great patience and a sense of humour.

Safe Journey!

1
Lagos

General

Lagos was the capital of Nigeria until the seat of government moved to the Federal Capital Territory at Abuja. Lagos has a life of its own and is completely different from other cities in Nigeria. It is the headquarters for many parastatals and national institutions. There is also a large commercial community, and a colourful Diplomatic Corps which adds a cosmopolitan flavour to the city.

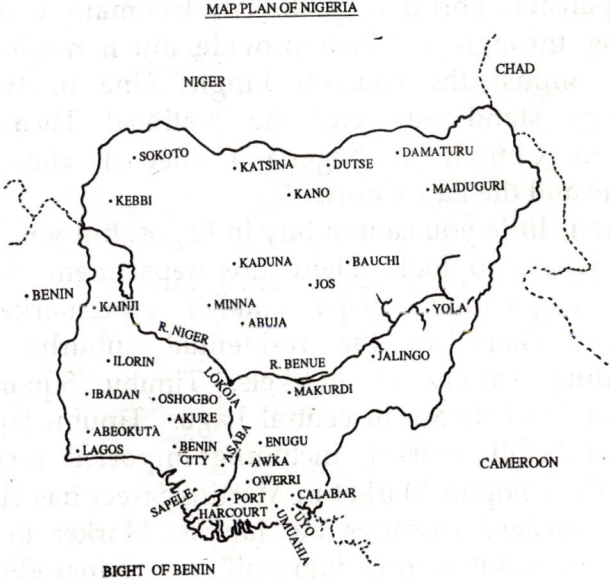

MAP PLAN OF NIGERIA

The city is a mass of human activity, day and night. Moving around is sometimes a slow and painful process, whether on foot or by car, owing to the hustle and bustle of so many people, all seemingly in an enormous hurry. Few vehicles do not carry signs of the bruising battles fought at every road junction, roundabout and bottleneck. It is a frenetic existence until the Lagosian gains the sanctuary of his own home. Some control over the traffic is gained by limiting the cars on the road on Mondays, Wednesdays and Fridays to those with numberplates beginning with odd numbers, and those on Tuesdays and Thursdays with numberplates beginning with even numbers.

Lagos still has many fine old colonial buildings both in the government and residential parts of the city, but many are now being replaced by large office blocks and flats, the necessary scourge of all modern cities with limited space for expansion. Fortunately, the city has many waterways running through it which provide much needed open spaces amidst the concrete jungle. One or two fine buildings stand out, e.g. the National Theatre, the Anglican Church of Nigeria Cathedral, the Central Mosque and the Law Courts.

There is little you cannot buy in Lagos, but you have to know where to look. There are department stores in central Lagos and Apapa, smaller supermarkets and specialist shops in the residential suburbs and a fascinating variety of markets. Tinubu Square and Balogun Markets are in central Lagos. Tinubu Square is the main cloth market, including imported furnishing materials. Balogun Market in Martins Street has clothing, shoes, jewellery, cassettes, etc. Jankara Market, in Okoya Street, has an interesting 'juju stall', where ingredients for traditional medicines are sold. Yaba has a large two-storeyed market building where you can also buy furnishing materials. Alaba Market along the Badagry Road sells a multitude of goods, including electrical and household goods, camera equipment and furniture. It is advisable not to be too ostentatious with money or jewellery when visiting these markets. For local handicrafts like carvings, baskets, beads, malachite, leatherware and cloth, there are traders' stalls outside the large hotels, but as usual, hard bargaining is essential. Recently, the old Bar Beach Market has been moved to a site along the Lekki Road amongst the new housing estate at the Lekki Beach roundabout. It sells tourist items, as well as fruits, vegetables, groceries and drinks. Apapa is a good shopping area as the large stores and the market are all nearby.

Near Lagos there are several sandy beaches along the Atlantic Coast which stretch for hundreds of kilometres to the east and west. However, there is a very strong undertow and great care must be taken as even strong swimmers have drowned on these beaches; so treat the sea with the greatest respect.

The wet season is longer in Lagos than in the north of Nigeria, and lasts from April to October with occasional storms outside this period. The hottest time is February to March, when the harmattan has usually receded and the rains have not begun.

Lagos is well-served by international and national airlines and has an expressway north to Ibadan and access to the Benin Expressway through either Sagamu or Epe. It is only a 2-hour drive to the border with the Benin Republic.

Tourist Sites

For a state capital, Lagos is not as well-endowed with tourist sites as some other cities in Nigeria. Nevertheless, the sites that should interest a tourist are:

1. **Art and Crafts**
   a. The National Museum, Onikan, near Tafawa Balewa Square. This museum is of great interest to any one interested in African art who wishes to understand the rich cultural heritage of Nigeria. Artefacts in the museum date back to 500BC–200AD in the case of the beautiful Nok terracotta heads. The museum is well-laid out to show the development of the various cultures throughout the centuries of Nigeria's history. Sometimes, the museum has exhibitions of art, and there is a craft village and museum kitchen at the back of the compound. It is open from 9.00 a.m. to 6.00 p.m. every day and prepares Nigerian dishes.
   b. National Gallery of Modern Art, National Theatre, Iganmu. Go in through entrance 'C'. Artwork from Nigeria's leading artists is on display. It is of interest to those who have not seen African art before as it is fascinating to see how the art forms differ from those in Europe and America. It is open from 9.00 a.m. until 5.00 p.m., Monday to Friday. At weekends you must apply to the management in writing one week in advance for it to be opened, but I suspect that it would be easier to go during the week.
   c. National Gallery of Crafts and Design, Opposite Gate 'C' of the National Theatre and is open from 9.00 a.m. until 5.00 p.m. except on weekends.
   d. The Didi Museum in Akin Adesola Street, is open from Monday to Saturday, 10.00 am until 5.00 pm. This small, privately-owned art collection, attractively displayed in a modern gallery, houses works of art by contemporary Nigerian artists as well as some African antiques, including bronzes, terracotta figures and wood carvings. The exhibits are changed frequently, to add variety.

2. **Beaches/Holiday Resort**

a. The main beach on Victoria Island is Victoria Beach, (usually known as Bar Beach) alongside Ahmadu Bello Road. It is very dangerous for swimming and it is not recommended. On public holidays it is crowded with Nigerians, who make a day of it, so it is a colourful scene, as people dress up for the occasion. It is not advisable to take valuables onto the beach. At present the beach is being gradually washed away by the sea but preventive measures were being taken in 1991 to save the beach.

b. Tarkwa Bay. A sheltered beach within the harbour break-water. You get there by a 'Tarzan' boat from Maroko, 'Fiki' boat from under Falomo Bridge, (Victoria Island end) or a boat from Paradise Holidays in Eleke Crescent. The beach is a pleasant outing and has safe bathing even for small children. You can hire deck chairs and an awning on the beach, and there are traders selling pineapples, coconuts and many other items. Take your own food, cold drinks and sun-cream. There are plenty of young boys to carry your possessions. Lighthouse Beach is beyond Tarkwa. It is a lovely open beach, but can be dangerous for swimming. Do not take jewellery, watches or cameras on the beach, especially if you walk away from the crowded areas.

c. Beaches along the Lekki Peninsula. The first, Lekki Beach, is only a few kilometres from the city. Take the road past the 1004 flats along the Maroko Road to the Lekki Peninsula, and at the third roundabout it is signposted to the right, along a new road. The charge is ₦5 for a car and ₦1 per person. It is possible to hire a beach shelter made of palmfronds. The bathing is dangerous, so great care must be taken. Unfortunately, the numerous traders tend to disturb your peace.

Maiyegun Beach is signed on the right just after the third roundabout. Access is along a sandy track which may not be suitable for all types of vehicles. The beach adjoins Lekki Beach and is similar to it in most aspects.

Eleko Beach was opened in 1989, and is further along the Lekki Peninsula, approximately 50 km from Lagos, just past the 'Epe 22' km post. It is signed to the right along a new sealed road which extends for 4 km to the beach. At the time of writing, this beach is quieter and there are fewer traders, but this situation may not last. There are other beaches, but these are only available by 4-wheel drive vehicles at present.

d. Badagry Beach is one hour's drive along the Badagry Road towards Cotonou in the Benin Republic. It is possible to go by boat to both Badagry and Agaja beaches, but the journey is expensive, unless you have your own boat.

e. Whispering Palms. This is a holiday resort located in Iworo town, in Badagry. It has facilities for decent accommodation, sporting, especially lagoon boating; recuperation and relaxation. The Whispering Palms Visa Card guarantees a free entry into the premises.

For more information, contact the booking office at Whispering Palms (Tenderloin Ltd.), First Floor, Leventis Stores Building, P.O. Box 951, Surulere, Lagos. Tel. (01) 849184.

Access is along the Lagos-Badagry Expressway and fork left after the toll gate. From this point, Iworo town is about 12 km away. Whispering Palms is located on the right side of the road. Watch out for gate with Bougainvillea.

3. Funfairs

A new leisure park called Happy land/Happy World is being built on the Lekki Peninsula on the Epe Road, approximately 29 km from Lagos. It is being set up by an American Company to include hotels, a sports complex, water park and a theme park modelled on Disney World in the USA. It is a vast project, planned for completion in 2011. Another funfair is planned to be built at Ikeja by the state government but the opening date is not yet known.

4. Gardens

Another new project on the Lekki Peninsula is the Murtala Muhammed Gardens dedicated to the memory of the late General, approximately 70 km from Lagos. The gardens were designed by the General's widow and opened by President Babangida in March 1991. They are signed on the right of the Epe Road coming from Lagos.

Hotels

The recommended hotels are:
a. Sheraton Hotel, Airport Road, Ikeja, Tel: 900931 (the Lagos code is 01). Said to be the best in Lagos, but it is some distance from the centre and the main residential area. Driving between the Sheraton and the main centres of commerce on Lagos Island can be slow and difficult, but the hotel is very convenient for the airport and the industrial areas of Ikeja. It has a swimming pool. The hotel meets international standards.
b. L'Hotel Eko Meridien (previously called Eko Holiday Inn), Kuramo Waters, Victoria Island, Tel: 615000. The most popular with overseas visitors, and recommended if you are visiting central Lagos. Has an excellent Chinese Restaurant on the top floor. There is a pleasant swimming pool.
c. The Federal Palace Hotel, Ahmadu Bello Way, Victoria Island. Tel: 610031. Has a good Italian

Restaurant in the basement, and a very good Chinese Restaurant in the main hotel.

d. The Ikoyi Hotel, Kingsway Road, Ikoyi. Tel: 603200. Also has a good Chinese Restaurant, which is not smart, but the food is very good.

None of these hotels are expensive for those paid in hard currencies, but not cheap if you are on the local economy. Most of the hotels have traders' stalls outside, where you can buy local handicrafts, but you need to bargain hard. Visitors without residence permits will have to pay their hotel bills in hard currency. There are restaurants to suit all tastes in Lagos. It is impossible to mention them all, but this is a selection.

a. The Brasserie, 52 Adetokunbo Ademola Street. Tel: 615464. There is continental cuisine on the ground floor and an Indian Restaurant on the first floor.

b. The Bagatelle: 208/212 Broad Street (fourth floor), Lagos Island, Tel: 662410. Excellent service.

c. Jaws Seafood Restaurant, Plot 8 Ozumba Mbadiwe Road, Victoria-Island. Mostly Chinese food.

d. The Lagoon, 1c Ozumba Mbadiwe, Victoria Island, Tel: 611616. Naturally, it overlooks the Lagoon, and the food is good.

e. The Sheraton, 108 Awolowo Road, which serves Indian food. Tel: 681911.

f. The Koreana, 81 Awolowo Road which serves Korean, Japanese and Chinese food. Tel: 681402.

g. The Water Gardens, 55 Awolowo Road, Chinese and Lebanese food. Tel: 681333.

Recommended books

The following books are recommended for more and detailed information about Lagos and its environ:

a. *Survive Lagos* by Elizabeth Cox and Erica Anderssen, Spectrum Books Ltd., Ibadan.

b. *Nigeria Tourist Guide,* obtainable from the Maison de France, Plot PC 14, off Idowu Taylor Street, Victoria Island. Tel:615592.

c. *Spectrum Road Map,* 1991 edition.

2

The South-west

General

South-west Nigeria covers the area bordered by the Benin Republic in the west, the River Niger in the north and east and the Gulf of Guinea/Bight of Benin in the south. The southern part of this region consists mainly of rain forest, oil palm and rubber plantations, the snaking rivers and mangrove swamps of the delta area and the long sandy beaches of the Atlantic coast. As you travel north towards the Niger the landscape changes slowly to guinea savanna, dotted with hills and inselberge (granite outcrops). This area includes some of the largest cities in Nigeria,

historical towns and shrines, a game reserve, some excellent museums, fascinating markets with some superb craftwork, besides many other places of interest.

South-west Nigeria also saw the first appearance of Europeans in the area, starting with the Portuguese in the 16th century followed by the palm-oil traders and English, Scottish and German missionaries who set up their first mission post at Badagry, west of Lagos in the 19th century. Sadly this area was also infamous for the slave trade which began before the appearance of the Europeans but was fully exploited by them. The trade, fortunately, was stopped by the British, but not without great suffering. Relics of the trade at the old slave posts are still to be seen along the coast, especially at Ouidah (pronounced Weedah) in the Benin Republic.

Abeokuta

General

Abeokuta is a Yoruba town with a mixed Christian and Muslim population. It is a historical town both for the Yoruba and for the early Christian missionaries who moved there from Badagry on the coast. The name Abeokuta, meaning 'under the rock', is derived from the Olumo Rock, which is the town's most famous landmark. Abeokuta is the capital of Ogun State and has a traditional ruler, the Alake of Egbaland. The town is built on the Ogun River between a number of rocky hills, and is therefore attractive photographically. It has several interesting markets and it is here that the traditional *adire* cloth is made.

Tourist sites

a. Olumo Rock. This rock, considered sacred by the

Egba people, is on the east side of the Ogun River, close to the centre of the town. When you reach the white-painted stone obelisk 'roundabout' near the market, turn right at the sign (north) and the entrance to the rocks is on the right a few hundred metres along this road. Everyone in Abeokuta knows where the rock is, so you can ask for directions. It is suggested that you take a guide from the tourist centre at the bottom of the rock, if they are available, who will show you the old living quarters in the caves used in the Yoruba civil wars as a sanctuary, and also conduct you to the top, where you can get an excellent view of Abeokuta and the Ogun River. There are steps to the caves and the shrine (where festivals are held and sacrifices offered), but after that the climb is fairly steep and it is essential to wear sensible shoes like trainers or desert boots. Take your camera as the scene from the summit is very impressive.

b. The Market. The local populace, the Egba, are keen traders. The market sells the traditional *adire* cloth which is made by a process similar to batik, but cassava starch is used instead of wax for applying the patterns and the material is then dyed in indigo, creating the beautiful blue and indigo cloth. Batik materials are also made at this market, using a variety of coloured dyes. The main cloth market is in the centre of the town; near the white stone obelisk.

c. Ijaye Pottery. The pottery stall is on the side of the road in the centre of the town, and has a large variety of interesting pots for sale. Ask in the market for directions.

d. The Oba's Palace. The official residence of the Alake of Egbaland is in Ake, a district of Abeokuta. On request you may be allowed to see around the palace, including the Throne Room which has a Bible presented by King Edward VII, and another by the present Queen of England. Wole Soyinka, the celebrated author who won the Nobel Prize for Literature (1986), was brought up in Ake where his father was a headmaster, and has given the name, Ake, to the first volume of his autobiography. It is a beautifully descriptive book.

Hotels

The Gateway International Hotel is the main hotel in Abeokuta and has a pleasant view of the town. There is a swimming pool and poolside bar for refreshments. A visit to Abeokuta can make a good day's outing from Lagos.

Route

The best route from Lagos is via the Ibadan Expressway. Turn off the expressway at Sagamu (about half-way), where it is signed to Abeokuta, and continue west until you reach the town. The journey takes less than 2 hours. To vary the route back to Lagos, take the old road, the A5 through Ifo, Ota and Ikeja. Both roads are good. Fruits and vegetables can be bought on the side of the road much more cheaply than in Lagos.

Abraka

General

Abraka is a tourist resort with a Motel, on the Ethiope River in Delta State about 100 km from Benin City. The crystal clear river which is fed by a spring, flows through a beautiful forested area. The Abraka River Resort Motel has a sandy beach on the river with tables and umbrellas, and you can hire boats to row yourself, or if you prefer, you can hire local canoes with a boy to paddle you upstream. It is fun to go up river and float back to the Motel in a rubber ring (inner tube) which can be hired from the Motel. The water is safe for swimming, and it is so clear that you can see the fish at the bottom 5m or so, below. There are several private beaches with beach huts along the river, belonging to large companies. A visit to Abraka is well worthwhile, especially with children, as you can have a safe swim and there is plenty to occupy both adults and children in an attractive setting.

Route

From Benin City, take the Sapele Road from the central roundabout. Just before Sapele, take the bypass road to the left and shortly after crossing a large bridge, turn left at the T-junction to Abraka. When you reach Abraka, the Motel is signed to the left down a sealed road. Journey time from Benin is about one and a half hours, but the road is currently being improved. Abraka is about five hours from Lagos.

Hotels

The Abraka River Resort Motel is right on the river with apartments and parking space for your car. There is also parking space for day visitors. At busy holiday periods the service can be rather slow. If you have children, it may be worth bringing some of their own favourite foods. Tel:(054)66140. Do take great care with your money and valuables.

Ayetoro Commune Village

General

Ayetoro Village was founded as a religious commune in 1945 and was once entirely self-supporting, with everything being owned collectively. Since the death of its leader, however, the community has been less structured, and now everything is owned individually. The village which is on the Ondo coastline, is interesting for its social history, but the appearance and atmosphere of the village is changing. Ayetoro (meaning 'world of peace') is on a strip of land between the sea and the lagoon and is connected by bridges which are necessary in the wet season. It can only be approached by boat from Igbo Koda, and the 55-minute journey in a fast boat is a very pleasant part of the outing, as much of the journey is through swamp forest and there are picturesque villages on stilts en route. Take a picnic lunch and plenty of water as well as hats and suncream for those with fair skin. It is a full day's outing from Lagos, so start early in the morning. Visitors are advised to pay a courtesy call on the Oba, or one of his staff.

Route

Drive east out of Victoria Island down the Lekki Peninsula to Epe and from there to the Benin Expressway at Ijebu Ode. Turn right onto the expressway and continue until you reach Ore (about 205 km). Turn right (south) and drive to Okitipupa (about 40 km). Just before the town, turn left at a T-junction with a statue of a boy carrying a bunch of palm kernels on his head. Turn right in Okitipupa where it is signed to Igbo Koda, and on reaching the village drive straight on until you reach the jetty where you hire a boat for the journey by water to Ayetoro. Negotiate the price for your journey before you start. In 1990, the best price was ₦200 per boat which could seat about 6-7 people, after hard bargaining. From Ikeja, the best way to the Benin Expressway is via the Ibadan Expressway and Sagamu.

Badagry

General

Badagry in Lagos State, on the coast, west of Lagos, was the first town settled by missionaries in Nigeria. The 'First Storey House' (the first two-storey building in the country) erected by the missionaries, is still standing and is due to be refurbished. The well-kept graveyard was the final resting place of missionaries from Scotland, England and Germany and you can still see their names on the gravestones. Most missionaries entered Nigeria from the east, through Calabar, but Badagry has the distinction of being the first mission post in the country. From here the missionaries moved north to Abeokuta. In the slave-trading days, many slaves were shipped from Badagry, and there are still some relics of this terrible trade in the town. Badagry, therefore, is of more interest to historians than the tourist. There are pleasant beaches nearby along the coast, but again, remember that the sea is dangerous and great care must be taken.

Route

From Lagos Island go round the National Theatre towards Festac Village and onto the Badagry Expressway. It is about 1 hour's journey in the direction of the border with the Benin Republic.

Benin City

General

Benin City (pronounced Beneen or Bini) is the capital of Edo State and is steeped in history. The world-renowned Benin bronzes date back to the 15th century when the Oba of Benin ruled the large and powerful Edo kingdom.

Bronze making was an art used for the glorification of the Oba. In 1897, a British expeditionary force sacked Benin and carried away many of the finest bronzes to London. This unfortunate incident was as a result of the ambush and murder of the British representatives on their way to visit the Oba in Benin. Consequently, the Oba was banished to Calabar, but the family was reinstated later by the British. The present Oba is a direct descendant. Some of the bronzes which were removed to England are on display in the British Museum where they are admired by people from all over the world, but there are several fine examples of the bronzes in both the Benin and Lagos Museums, especially the latter. Today, bronze-making is still continued in several streets in the city.

Tourist sites

a. The Oba's Palace is in the centre of the city, south-west of the central roundabout and it is possible to visit it if a request is made to the Oba's secretary. Festivals are held here throughout the year, but the most important, the Igue, is during the last two weeks of December.It is normally held in the evening.

b. The Benin Museum is situated in the middle of the large central roundabout in the city. It contains examples of the famous bronzes and other historical artefacts. It is open daily from 9.00 am. to 6.00 p.m. including Sundays. It is proposed to open a Museum kitchen serving Nigerian food.

c. Bronze craft. There are several streets where bronze making by the 'lost wax' process is still practised, including Igun and Oloton Streets. Igun Street is first left off Sakpoba Road, just past Leventis Stores at the central roundabout. Samson Aigbe's workshop is on the left, in Igun Street. Billy Omodamwen's Art

Gallery and Workshop is at 7, Oloton Street, off Oba Market Road, Tel. (052) 246814. This is both a traditional bronze workshop by a master of the art and a tourist shop.

d. Wood-carvers. Again, there are several streets where wood-carvers are to be found, but the main one is on the Airport Road, close to the Oba's Palace. One of the best is the Edo Carving Centre, 14 Airport Road, Tel. (052) 240768. The Managing Director is Mr W.A. Agho.

e. Oba's market This is an extensive market near the Oba's Palace. All the above places of interest are conveniently situated in the centre of the town near the central roundabout.

f. Chief Ogiamen's House. This is situated at 97 Sakpoba Road, which is off the central roundabout. As the sign outside his house says, 'This is a fine example of Benin traditional architecture built before 1897'. It is unique in that no building of a comparable status survived intact the Great Fire which occurred at the time and destroyed a great part of the city.' It is possible to obtain permission to visit this house through the curator of the museum, or the Chief himself if he is in residence.

g. Benin Moat. Originally the town was defended by a deep moat, stretching right round the city, parts of which are still visible today, and would be of interest to historians. There are plans to renovate these very significant earthworks.

h. Ebohon Cultural Centre. This is well worth a visit for it is a centre for traditional African religion, culture, arts and crafts. It include shrines, a herbal garden, a hospice for traditional medicine, and a dance troupe is attached to the centre. It is interesting to visit the Ebohon Centre and experience the work of the Chief

Priest, Ebohon. The centre is at 1 Odenede Street, near Sakpoba Street and is open from 9 a.m. to 2 p.m. and 5 p.m. to 7 p.m. Monday to Saturday and on Sunday from 7 p.m. to 9 p.m. Address. P O Box 223 Benin City, Tel. (052) 242174 or 222081.

Route

From Lagos, the journey takes about three and a half hours. From Victoria Island or Ikoyi the best route is along the Lekki Peninsula to Epe, then to Ijebu Ode where you turn right onto the Benin Expressway. Continue for over 200 km until you reach Benin City. From Ikeja, take the Ibadan Expressway to Sagamu and turn right onto the Benin Expressway.

Guide

If you want a guide, Mr John Igbinakpogie from the Ministry of Education may be of help. Tel. (052) 229281.

Hotels

The Country Home Hotel, The Ranch: This is about 7 km from the central roundabout along the Sapele Road, on the outskirts of the city. There is a large signboard on the right of the road just past an Agip Petrol Station. Turn right and the hotel is on the left, about 0.5 km up the road. It has motel type accommodation with parking outside. Tel. (052) 244641 or 244394.

The Saidi Centre in Murtala Muhammad Way (between Sapele and Sakpoba roads) is Lebanese run, and the restaurant has Lebanese and Chinese foods. Some new accommodation was completed in 1991. The food is good and Mr Saidi himself is often there to supervise the running of the hotel. Tel. (052) 242125.

The Emotan Hotel is at 1 Central Road, in the GRA and

has recently been refurbished. Tel. (052) 200130–2.

Other tourist sites

a. Abraka (*see* page 13).

b. The Nana's Palace at Koko on the coast is a worthwhile place to visit. Unfortunately, Koko recently received adverse publicity due to the dumping of toxic chemical waste in 1988. However, it has since been removed and there should no longer be any danger to visitors.

c. Source of the Ethiope River at Umutu near Abraka. There is a spring, and a 'Juju' tree which is known for its large quantity of frogs.

d. Okomu Forest Reserve. The reserve is near Udo, west of Benin City. This reserve contains some of the last remaining rainforest in Nigeria, which is being preserved with the help of the Nigerian Conservation Foundation (NCF). It still has a herd of forest elephants and is home to the white-faced monkey, which is indigenous to Nigeria only. The forest is an excellent place to see birds and butterflies. A 150 ft high observation platform has been constructed in a tree, for those with a good head for heights. Permission to visit the reserve is usually sought first from the NCF, 5, Mosley Road, Ikoyi, Lagos, Tel: (01) 686163 or 687385. There is a Guest House belonging to the African Timber and Plywood (AT & P) in the Reserve but again, permission to use it must be obtained from AT & P or its parent company, the United Africa Company (UAC). Alternative accommodation, one hour's journey away, is at the Okada Wonderland which is signed to the left off the

Benin Expressway. Okada Wonderland has chalets with children's play parks, fish ponds and a Garden of Honour with cement statues of famous people. The accommodation is adequate.

e. Jakpa is a village on the Benin River not far from the coast, which has a history of early exploration and trade. Only approached by boat.

f. Old Warri: *see* Warri on page 48.

Erin Ijesa Falls

Erin Ijesa is a series of 7 waterfalls in Osun State between Akure and Ilesa. The path to the bottom fall is only about 0.5km from the car-park, and an easy walk. From there though, the path to the top is very steep, a fork to the right leads to the second fall from where there is a good view of the falls. The left fork has smaller paths leading to different stages of the falls, but finally comes out onto the 'plateau'. This walk is only for the fit and agile! The area round the first fall is forested and cool and a pleasant place for a picnic, with benches to sit on, and easily accessible to the less agile.

Route

From Akure, the capital of Ondo State, take the Akure-Ilesa Road. About 50 km from the outskirts of Akure there is a turning to the right marked 'To Erin Oke'. Go through the village of Erin Oke turning left at the T-junction just beyond the main road and proceed about 2 km into Erin Ijesa along the main street. At the church and police station, take the right fork and almost immediately afterwards, turn right again where there is a sign to the falls. The car park is about 1 km further on, at the foot of the hills. It is at least a 4-hour drive from Lagos and it is best to make it a weekend trip, staying at Akure or Ibadan. There is an alternative route a few kilometres further along the main road, with a sign to the falls, but it is not obvious.

Hotels

The Owena Motel in Parliament Road, Akure is adequate. Coming from Ondo, turn left in Akure at the compulsory left sign and then right at the T-junction onto the dual carriageway. Proceed about $1\frac{1}{2}$ km and turn right at the "Owena Motels Ltd." sign and left at the next junction by the NEPA building. Straight on, at the next roundabout and shortly after, turn right into the Motel. Tel. (034) 232560. A good alternative is the Akure Plaza Hotel, Tel. 232075 or 231211 (*see* page 25).

Ibadan

General

Ibadan is said to be the largest city in black Africa. It is the capital of Oyo State and is in the heart of Yorubaland. The University of Ibadan, abbreviated as UI, is the premier University in Nigeria. There are many seats of learning in Ibadan including a Teaching Hospital, the International Institute for Tropical Agriculture (IITA), the Cocoa Research Institute and the Federal Agricultural Research Institute.

Tourist sites

a. The University and its bookshop. There is also a stall selling *adire* cloth and some jewellery.
b. Ibadan Zoo—in the grounds of the University near the Zoology Department. The zoo is small but children would enjoy it. The reptile house is of special interest.
c. There are several large markets in Ibadan, one of which, the Oje Market, has a large section selling items for traditional medicines. *Aso oke* cloth, woven

by men on narrow looms is also sold in the Ibadan market area.

d. The International Institute for Tropical Agriculture, (IITA), has a beautiful estate and many excellent facilities: a swimming pool, tennis courts, 9-hole golf course, squash court, a lake for fishing, excellent bird watching and a forest walk. However, it is not open to the public and permission must be obtained before visiting it.

Route

From Lagos there is a direct route via the Lagos-Ibadan Expressway, but you can try taking a slower and more interesting journey up the old road to Ibadan from Lagos. The A1 through Ikorodu-Sagamu-Ajebo will give you more atmosphere than the busy expressway.

Hotels

The Premier Hotel is an option but many make Ibadan a day trip from Lagos. The Premier Hotel is an obvious landmark—a multi-storey white building on top of a hill not far from the Secretariat or Government buildings. It is also the largest hotel in Ibadan. There is an excellent view of the town from the hotel, but an alternative is the new (1988) Kakanfo Inn which is Indian-managed. It is just off the Ring Road near the road to Abeokuta. Go up Adebiyi Street popularly called Joyce B Road and it is on the left. Another new hotel is the D' Rovans Hotel along Ibrahim Babangida way.

Idanre

General

The modern Yoruba town of Idanre in Ondo State is set in a valley surrounded by magnificent inselbergs rising to about 900m. (Inselbergs are granite hills left standing above the surrounding countryside by the erosion of softer ground around them.) Old Idanre is the original village, said to be 800 years old, which lies in a hanging valley reached by some 442 concrete steps. It was finally abandoned in 1933 although the Owa (Oba) still lives there for part of the year, and his palace is used for ceremonial occasions. Guides will take you up the steps to the village. There are resting places on the way up and at the top of the steps there are three rest houses (closed) but they have shady verandahs, and there is a magnificent view of the town from this point (best photographed with a wide-angled lens.) From there to the old village and the Owa's palace it is either a pleasant 15-minute walk along a shady path or a short scramble over the rocks. The Owa's palace has a fine courtyard with carved figures and doors. There is a shrine containing animal skulls and bones.

A further climb to a higher peak will bring you to various sacred sites, the mysterious mat and a magical footprint in the rock that is said to fit any foot that does not belong to a witch. The Owa of Idanre traces the origin of his people through Oduduwa back to Egypt. The strange footprint is ascribed to that of Agbogun, the first son of Olofin, brother of Oduduwa who founded Idanre. (*See* page 27 on Ile Ife for more about Oduduwa. It is possible also to climb to the meterological station at the top of the hill, which takes about another 40 minutes to get to the top. The first part is through forest, then a steep walk up the bare rock. There are magnificent views from the summit but this is definitely only for the very fit. (*See* Erin Ijesa on page 21 for something else to do while in the area.) Allow $2\frac{1}{2}$ to 3 hours for the climb up and back to Old Idanre, with stops for refreshments. Local boys will guide you and carry your picnic things. Negotiate a price before engaging them.

Route

The route from Lagos is along the Lekki dual carriageway to Epe, north to the Benin Expressway, then turn right along the expressway to Ore, (or alternatively via Ikeja and Sagamu). At Ore, turn left (north) to Ondo. The road to Idanre is marked to the right about 23 km from Ondo on the Akure Road. There is also a road from Akure: turn south off the main road at the Post Office, and after passing the Oba's palace, take the first right, then first left, which is the Idanre Road.

Hotels

The nearest place to stay is the Owena Motel Akure which is adequate. Coming from Ondo turn left in Akure at the compulsory left sign and then right at the T-junction. Turn right at the 'Owena Motels Ltd'. signed about $1\frac{1}{2}$ km along the road, and left at the NEPA building. Straight on, at the next roundabout and shortly afterwards, turn right into the motel.

Another good alternative is the Akure Plaza Hotel which the Nigerian Field Society uses. Go left off the dual carriageway (Adesina Road) onto Oke Ijebu Road. Go for a few kilometres to Plaza road. Follow the signs to the Plaza Hotel. It is well managed and helpful. Tel. (034) 232075 or 231211.

Ijebu Ode Birikisu-Sungbo Shrine, Oke Eri

General

The shrine, which is located near Ijebu Ode (pronounced I-je-bu-ode), at Oke Eri, is the tomb of Birikisu, a noblewoman of note whom legend says became one of the wives of King Solomon, and therefore a 'Queen of Sheba'. It is said that Birikisu was such a powerful woman that she dug wells with the aid of needles. The shrine is a religious monument for Muslims in Nigeria, and only *men* are allowed access to the tomb. It was said that a European woman once disregarded this advice and stepped onto the tomb. She is believed to have died in an accident soon afterwards. It is claimed that although the tomb is under the trees, no leaves fall on the tomb itself. In summary, the shrine is of great significance to Muslims, but is not a tourist site as such. Permission to enter it must first be obtained from the caretaker, and you will be asked to remove your shoes. Ask for the caretaker in the village of Oke Eri. In 1990 the charge was ₦10.

Route

Ijebu Ode is an hour's journey from Lagos just off the Benin Expressway. Either take the Lekki Peninsula Road to Epe and then north to Ijebu Ode which is opposite the turn-off onto the expressway, or go north on the Ibadan Expressway and thence to the Benin Expressway. Go into Ijebu Ode and take the Ibadan Road. Shortly afterwards turn right to Oke Eri just after a Felico Filling Station.

Hotels

The Debasco Holiday Inn, at Atiba near Ijebu Ode on the road to Itoikin, was opened in May 1989. It has motel-style apartments, a conference hall, a disco and a tennis court. It is not connected to NEPA yet, so it uses a generator. The chalets have self-catering kitchens as there is no restaurant.

Ikogosi Warm Springs

General

The Ikogosi Warm Springs are at the village of Ikogosi (not marked on most maps), under an hour's drive from Akure. The actual springs are not of great significance, as

The Ooni of Ife

The Osun Shrine, Osogbo

The Anglican Cathedral, Lagos Island

Benin bronzes

View of the modern town of Idanre

A kob in Kainji Lake National Park, Borgu Sector

Fulani girl, Kwara State

Pied kingfisher *(Ceryle rudis)*

the warm water bubbles out from a rock, forming a stream only a few inches deep. It meets with a cold water stream 100 m below. However, there is a swimming pool with warm water from the springs. There is also a very small 'Zoological Garden' beside the springs. These springs are only worth visiting if you are in the area, but it could be combined with a visit to the Ipole-Iloro water cataracts, which are 6 km north of Ikogosi.

Route

From Akure take the Ilesa Road and after approximately 22 km there is a turning to the right at Igbara Oke towards Igbara Odo by a Coca Cola advert. Proceed for about $1\frac{1}{2}$ km into Igbara Odo, turn left, after another 1 km, turn right by a sign pointing to Ikogosi Motel. Drive 13 km to Igbara Odo and turn left and immediately right into the village. At the T-junction, turn right and drive about 20 km to Ikogosi Ekiti. In this town, drive straight through the junction, past the motel, and the road to the Warm Springs is on the right at the fork.

Hotels

See Idanre on page 25 for directions to the Owena Motel at Akure. The tourist board have now built chalets at the Ikogosi Warm Springs. Warm water is supplied direct from the warm springs.

Ile Ife

General

Ile Ife, in Osun State, is a unique city. To the Yorubas, it is the cradle of creation and civilisation and their legendary religious home. The legend says that it was at Ife that Oduduwa, sent from heaven by Olodumare, the Yoruba creator-God, established the first land upon the waters which then covered the earth, thus, becoming the founder of Ife. His sons spread to other parts of Yorubaland to create further kingdoms (*see* Idanre on page 23).

Ile Ife became a remarkable centre for arts, producing both terracotta figures and bronzes, dating from between the 12th and 15th centuries, and second only in fame to the Benin bronzes. Later, Ife declined in importance owing to the upheaval caused by the Fulani wars, and lost the art of bronze-making. The origins of Ife art still continue to baffle scholars, but it is thought that the bronzes were funeral effigies and the terracotta heads were used for the cult of ancestor worship and for shrine furniture. It was not until 1910 when a German, Leo Frobenius, took some of these figures to Germany, that this sophisticated African art-form was seen in Europe. Some of the figures have since been returned.

Tourist sites

a. The Museum. This is next to the Ooni's Palace, in the centre of the town, on Iremo Street. Here you can see the famous head of Olokun, the sea goddess, a representation of which is now the emblem of the Obafemi Awolowo University. The museum is small, but of great interest to those interested in African art, with its collection of terracotta heads, bronze figures and wood carvings. Some of the most significant artworks from Ile-Ife can also be seen in the National Museum in Lagos.

b. The Ooni of Ife's Palace. This is situated in the centre of the city on Iremo Street. The Ooni is the traditional ruler of Ile Ife and according to Yoruba tradition, is descended from Oduduwa. It is possible to visit the Palace, but only if permission is sought first from the Ooni's secretary.

c. Opa Oranyan (sometimes spelt Oranmiyan). This is

an engraved monolith about 5 m tall standing in a sacred grove south of the Palace off Iyekere Street, said to belong to the giant Oranyan. It was said to have been used in the defence of Ife against its enemies and to have been turned to stone on the achievement of victory. Visitors may see and photograph the staff, but should not proceed further up the path to the shrine, as this might cause offence. In Ife there are several sacred groves with shrines but permission should be sought before visiting them, and a guide hired. Ask at the museum for information.

d. University of Ife. The Obafemi Awolowo University, as it is now called, was established in 1962 and moved to Ife in 1967. It is on the Ibadan road a few kilometres before Ile Ife and has extensive grounds, with a park and a lake. The Institute of African Studies has been moved to the university campus from the town, and has a gallery for contemporary Nigerian artists, but unfortunately it is not open at the weekend.

Route

From Lagos, Ile Ife is best approached from Ibadan. Leave the expressway where the road is marked to Ife, and continue along the A12 to the town, which is 86 km from Ibadan.

Hotels

The Hotel Diganga, which is on the left hand side of the road coming from Ibadan, near the entrance to the University, is suitable for an overnight stay, but you can make it a day-trip from Lagos. The journey takes about 3 hours each way. The Conference Centre on Road 8, OAU, Ile Ife also has rooms and has been recommended. An alternative is the Concord Holiday and Health Farm

Resort at Ilesa, half an hour from Ife, which is reasonable. Tel. (036) 460872-78

Ilorin

General

The ancient city of Ilorin is the capital of Kwara State. It is often described as the gateway between the northern and southern parts of the country because of its strategic location. It is a good base for visiting the surrounding area which has many tourist sites.

Tourist sites

a. Alfa Alimi's Mosque and Residence—the mosque and residence were built in 1831. It was the first mosque in Ilorin. Alfa Alimi was a Fulani Muslim scholar sent by the Sokoto Caliphate to propagate Islam to the people of Ilorin. He also played a part in the disintegration of the Old Oyo Empire. Ask for the mosque, which is of historical value only and is in the back streets behind the Emir's palace which is beside the Central Mosque.

b. Okuta Ilo Irin (stone for sharpening metal tools) at Asaju's Compound at Idiape Quarters close to the Emir's palace. This is the stone on which one of the founders of Ilorin, known as Ojo Isekuse, used to sharpen his metal tools. The town derived its name from the use to which the stone was put. In the past, the stone was worshipped with sacrificial offerings, but this is no longer the case.

c. Dada Pottery Workshop in the Okelele quarter of Ilorin. It is one of the largest traditional pottery factories in the country. There is also calabash workshop at 91 Azeez Atta Road, opposite the Baptist Church in the Surulere District of Ilorin.

Other local tourist sites

a. Esie Museum of Stone Figures has approximately 1,000 soap-stone figures of men and women sitting on stools. The stools are significant in having circular tops and bases joined by columns. There are some kneeling figures of both sexes with elaborate hair-styles and facial markings. Little is known about them except that they come from a very old civilisation. The museum houses the largest collection of stone images in Black Africa.

Esie is near Oro on the Ilorin-Lokoja Road, a few kms past the town of Ajasse which is 42 km from Ilorin. At Oro, turn right off the main road into the town at a petrol station on the top of the hill. Turn left at the T-junction and take the right fork at the small square. Esie is the adjoining village across a small bridge, and the sign to the museum is just short of the village pointing to the right. It is about 2 km further, at the end of the road.

b. Igbeti town. This is the ancient city of the Oyo Obas. It is worth a visit if you are passing, but probably not worth a special expedition.

Route

To get to Ilorin take the expressway to Ibadan, continue north along the A1 through Oyo and Ogbomoso on a busy winding road to Ilorin. It is just over 300 km from Lagos, so allow at least 4 to $4\frac{1}{2}$ hours.

Hotels

The Kwara Hotel is the recommended hotel in Ilorin, but it has not been well maintained. The Chinese restaurant in the hotel serves excellent food. As you reach Ilorin, fork right at the AP garage. Turn right between the Total garage and the Fire Station, turn left at the next roundabout along the dual carriageway, and first right up the hill, Ahmadu Bello Avenue. Go straight on at the next roundabout and the Kwara Hotel is on the left after the government offices. Tel: (031) 221490. An alternative is the Circular Hotel in New Yidi Road. Tel:(031) 220845.

Iseyin

General

Iseyin is a good base for exploring this beautiful and unspoilt area of south-west Nigeria.

Tourist sites

a. Narrow Loom Weaving. There are a number of weavers around the town. They are to be found in compounds in the centre of the town, behind Iseyin market.
b. The Nigerian Tobacco Company (NTC) plant nursery. They have a large selection of garden plants available at competitive prices.
c. Ogboro Inselberg. Take the Saki Road and fork right at Ago-Are, then a left turn at Sepeteri. A guide (possibly carrying a long danegun) will take you up the inselberg having gained permission from the Oba of Ogboro (a bottle of spirits is the best *laisser-passer*). The climb is stiff. An old fortified village is at the summit. Baboons and monkeys may also be seen and on climbing down you go through defiles and bat-infested caves. Ogboro is about 100 km north of Iseyin along a poor road, so allow plenty of time for the journey.
d. Ado Awaye Inselberg. Take the Abeokuta Road out of Iseyin, heading south-west. After about 26 km you will reach Ado Awaye village. The Chief's permission

The best times for game viewing are in the early morning or evening, and trips can be arranged from 6.00 am either in park vehicles or your own vehicle. Bird life is abundant, especially near the river, but animals are less often seen than at Yankari and game reserves in East Africa.

Visitors should call at the Wawa Game Warden's office (18 km from New Bussa) to be briefed and to book a game guide. The entrance to the reserve is approximately 30 km from Wawa along a laterite road, and the Oli River Camp is a further 50 km from the entrance.

c. Wildlife Trophies Museum/Restaurant. This is at the office premises at Wawa. The museum is small but may be worth a visit, especially for children. The restaurant serves local food, soft-drinks and beer. Game reserve T-shirts are on sale in the shop.

d. Uwuru Rapids. The Uwuru Rapids were on the Niger River south of the dam, but are now covered by water as a result of the Jebba Dam.

Other tourist sites

You may wish to explore further north from Wawa towards Yelwa and the Niger ferry to the north of the Kainji Lake. There are various Kamberi villages along the route, which have interesting markets on different days of the week. The road is laterite and badly corrugated.

Route

The route from Lagos is via Ibadan-Ilorin bypass (turn left at the sign to Jebba between Ogbomoso and Ilorin)-Jebba-Mokwa. At Mokwa, turn left (west) to Kainji and new Bussa just before you reach the town. The distance from Lagos to New Bussa, where there is a motel, is about 543 km. This can be done in a day, but some may prefer to break their journey en route. If you are staying at the Oli River Camp, (which is approximately 100 km further), take the third exit off the roundabout at New Bussa, heading north-west, to Wawa (18 km). Turn left when you reach the T-junction and the game reserve office is about 100 m on the right. Here you can pick up a guide for the 80 km to the camp, which is all on untarred roads and can take up to 2 hours. Petrol can be obtained from Oli River Camp, but it would be wise to have a reserve supply.

Hotels

At New Bussa the Kainji Motel is the recommended accommodation. It has 4 VIP suites and 40 double rooms. The motel is adequate but there is no choice of food. It is not expensive but be prepared for fairly basic living. If you have children, it would be wise to take some of their favourite food to supplement the fare. The swimming pool was not in use on our visit. From the roundabout turn right, then take the third large turning on the left (3 km). Continue along this road until it curves to the right, and the Kainji Motel is on your right.

The Oli River Lodge inside the reserve is only open from December to June. It provides reasonable accommodation and a simple restaurant, and is a good base inside the park from which to go game viewing. The rooms have air-conditioners but the generator is only used at night. As it is on the Oli River there is a good bird-watching area around the camp. However, take some protection against the tsetse flies.

Lokoja

General

Lokoja is the capital of Kogi State and is an historic town, due to its position at the confluence of the two great rivers, the Niger and the Benue. It became the headquarters of the Royal Niger Company in the 19th century. Lord Lugard, who brought the north of Nigeria under British control, had his quarters at Lokoja, which are still standing. These were pre-fabricated buildings and no nails were used in their construction. Bishop Samuel Ajayi Crowther, the first African bishop in Nigeria, also lived in Lokoja. Another 'first' was the founding of Holy Trinity School in 1865, the earliest primary school in the country. There is an 'Iron of Liberty'—the iron which slaves could touch to regain their freedom, inside the compound of this school. The graveyard contains the graves of some of the Northern Emirs exiled to Lokoja after Lord Lugard's campaign, and several British servicemen and colonial officers. There is a fine memorial to the Nigerian soldiers who were killed in the two world wars. Lokoja is perhaps of more interest to the historian rather than the tourist, but there is a magnificent view of the confluence of the two rivers from the top of Mount Patti up a very steep hill behind the town. Take the laterite track opposite the Plaza Hotel, although this is definitely only suitable for 4-wheel drive vehicles, but would make an excellent walk for the energetic. Unfortunately, many of the historical places in Lokoja are not obvious and to find them needs determination and patience. Possibly one of the older citizens might be persuaded to act as a guide.

Route

From Lagos, the most direct route is via the Benin Expressway to Ore, then turn left and go through Ondo,

Akure and a few kilometres past the Owo bypass (on the Ifon Road), take a turning to the left along a new road at Ipele which goes directly to Kabba and then on to Lokoja. An alternative route is through Benin City and Auchi.

Hotels

The recommended hotel is the Plaza Hotel, 3 Mt. Patti Road, Lokoja GRA, which could be used if you need a stop between Lagos and Abuja. There is a Catering Rest House nearby which has seen better days, but was being repainted in 1991.

Offa

This is a small town 50 km south of Ilorin, near Esie, and might be worth a visit if you are going to the Museum at Esie. The Olofa of Ofa has a traditional palace here and the late Olofas have a tomb in the town. The Onimoka Shrine and the Afelele Lake may also be of interest. The Onimoko Yam Festival is held around July/August and is an exciting festival featuring a wrestling combat between the traditional ruler and his second-in-command, the ceremonial cutting of the new yam, and cultural dancing.

Route

From Ilorin take the Lokoja Road to Ajasse and then turn right (south) towards Ofa, or approach from Osogbo in the south, but either way, part of the road was in poor condition in 1990.

Okomu Forest Reserve *(See* Benin City on page 16)

Omo Forest

General

This is the Ogun State Forestry Plantation Project north of the Benin Expressway, about 2 hours journey from Lagos. It can only be entered with permission from the manager of the project, Office J4, Box 2068, Ijebu Ode. It is mentioned in this guide as it is of special interest to naturalists and ornithologists. There are bird-watching sites, primary forest (rapidly being cut down), a bailey bridge over the Sasa River and a pleasant lake with a boat-house. The Forestry Project has chalets which can be hired on application and there is a club house with a wide verandah for picnics, but it has no staff or facilities. The Nigerian Field Society (NFS) sometimes organises trips to this forest, and it would be best to contact a member to guide you, but remember to obtain permission first.

Route

From Lagos take the road along the Lekki Peninsula to Epe, and then to Ijebu Ode. Turn right onto the Benin Expressway and continue for approximately 30 km until you see a wide laterite road on your left at the top of a hill. (Coming from the Benin direction, turn right near the 'Sagamu 78 km' post.) Continue on the road, through two barriers and turn right to the lake past the staff houses. If you should drive further into the forest, use a compass and take a note of your route, as it is easy to get lost. All roads look the same inside the forest! It is better to be guided on the first occasion. (From Ikeja or mainland Lagos, take the Ibadan Expressway to Sagamu and turn right onto the Benin Expressway. The turn-off is 30 km past the Fari Petrol Station at Ijebu Ode).

Osogbo

General

Osogbo is the capital of Osun state, created in 1991. It was the site of the great battle between the Fulani invaders from the north and the Yoruba armies of the south in 1838-9, in which the Fulani were decisively defeated. Legend gives much credit for their defeat to the river goddess, Osun, who is supposed to live in the river near the shrine. An Austrian-born artist, Suzanne Wenger, has done much to revive the cult of Osun in recent years, and with the help of Yoruba artists, has created strange and interesting cement sculptures and carvings. There is an extensive area to visit in a peaceful forest setting. The shrine itself is near the river, and from the old iron bridge nearby there is a pleasant view of the river. There are other sacred areas across the road with dramatic sculptures, including one depicting elephants and another a market. There are guides who will show you round for a small charge. You may also be asked to contribute money at the shrine itself. Suzanne Wenger still lives in Osogbo (1992) and her house is also decorated with sculptures. There is a small craft shop in her house, which is in the centre of the town. From the green and red mosque turn left at the 'Marlboro' traffic box and then first right. Her house is on the left going down the hill.

Osogbo town is famous for its arts and crafts: painting, wood carving, decorated calabashes and batik dyeing. The artist, Twin Seven Seven, one of the best-known artists of Osogbo, and Nike Davies who has exhibited her batiks in London and New York, both live on the old Ede Road. Twin Seven Seven, who is also a musician, lives opposite the Grammar School and Nike's Centre for Arts and Culture is on the right a little further out of Osogbo. The centre has batiks, *adire* cloth quilts, art works, carvings and a cultural dance troupe, so it is well worth a visit. The telephone number of the Nike Centre is (035) 234484. It is probably best to visit Osogbo as part of a tour with the Nigerian Field Society, or some other cultural society in order to have a guided tour of the various art centres: Suzanne Wenger's House and St. Joseph's Workshop. The latter is some kilometres north of Osogbo, and produces excellent wood carvings. The town has many artists' studios, but the above are among the best.

Route

From Lagos, take the expressway to Ibadan and then turn off where it is signed to Ife. However, once on the roundabout, take the second exit towards Iwo which will take you direct to Osogbo on a good new road. To reach the Osun shrine, you turn right at the junction when reaching Osogbo, follow the course of the roundabout and veer left up the hill. Move on until you reach the large green and red Central Mosque. Turn right again and carry on for 2 km until you reach the shrine. This is indicated by the sculptures beside the road. The entrance to the shrine is on the left beside a small car park.

Hotels

The Osun Presidential Hotel, Old Ikirun Road, (Tel: 035-232399) is a satisfactory stopover if you wish to stay in Osogbo, but Ibadan is only an hour's journey away. You can make it a day trip from Lagos if you start early in the morning, as the journey takes 3 hours each way. Ibadan is less than an hour's journey away.

Ososo

Ososo is a small village in the very north of Edo State, 20 km from Okene, where a Guest House has been built on top of a rock with a magnificent view. However, when we visited it in 1991, it had not yet been furnished, but hopefully this may be remedied in the future.

Owo

General

Owo is an old Yoruba town which was originally walled. It is now notable for its small, but interesting, collection of Yoruba sculptures in the local museum in front of the Olowo's palace. These were excavated in 1971. The Olowo's palace is the largest in Yorubaland, covering a 99 hectare piece of land to the west of the town. There were over 100 ancient courtyards of which 17 are still reasonably intact.

Route

Lagos-Benin Expressway to Ore, turn left to Ondo and Akure. Owo is less than 1 hour's drive east from Akure. Turn right at the turning from the main Akure Road into the centre of the town and right again up a small slope. The Olowo's palace is on the right with ample parking space. Ask, if there is any doubt. Everyone knows the Olowo's palace.

Hotels

There is no suitable hotel. It is better to stay at the Owena Motel or Akure Plaza in Akure. For directions to the motel, see Idanre on page 25.

Owu Falls (or Ore Falls)

General

Owu Falls in Kwara State is the highest and most spectacular natural waterfall in West Africa. Naturally, it is at its most spectacular in the wet season. The fall cascades 100 m down an escarpment with rocky outcrops, to a pool of ice-cold water below. The path leads right to the pool alongside a tree-lined stream. The views en route to the town of Owa Kajola are scenic and the escarpment is a very impressive sight.

Route

The falls are about 95 km from Ilorin. At Ilorin take the Lokoja Road (A123) for about 61 km until you reach the village of Oke-Inigbin (shortly before Omu-Aran), where the falls are signed to the left (north). Take a laterite road for 11 km to Isanlu-Isin, turn left at the T-junction, and continue to the village of Owa Kajola (28 km), turning left at the sign to the falls near a church. At the end of the road, follow the track on foot for about 2 km. (The distance from the main road is about 33 km in all.) In April 1990, a bulldozer was enlarging the track, and there were plans to tar the road, but it was still necessary to ford a stream on the road beyond Owa Kajola which may be impassable in the wet season until it is bridged.

Hotels

See Ilorin on page 31 for information on hotels.

Patani

Patani is on the west bank of the River Forcardos, one of the major branches of the Niger River after it divides into several rivers in the delta region. It is on the main Warri-Port Harcourt Road and there is a motel on the bank of the river which, although little used, can make a useful picnic spot on a journey. The bar serves cold drinks and for a small charge you can eat your picnic in pleasant surroundings. It could possibly be used as an overnight stop as it has chalets. There are pleasant views of the river from the motel.

Route to the Motel

From Warri take the Port Harcourt Road, and approximately 2 km before the large bridge at Patani there is a small road to the right. Continue along this road (roughly parallel with the main road) for 2 km until you reach a T-junction near the river. Turn right and the motel is on the left through some large metal gates. It has pleasant views of the river traffic (the local ferries and fishermen), and an imposing bridge over the River Forcardos.

Pategi

Pategi is on the River Niger in Kwara State, and is known for its regattas when the Nupe people from Pategi and Bida have fishing, swimming and canoeing competitions on the river. The long canoes are manned by many paddlers, and it is a spectacular sight. The date of the festival is not fixed. It is necessary to make enquiries from the local area or go to the Kwara State Liaison Office in Victoria Island, Lagos, for information. Pategi is also known for the carving of wooden doors. It is suggested that Ilorin is used as a base.

Route

From Ilorin, take the Lokoja Road until you reach Egbe. From there it is approximately 60 km to the north, much of it along a rough laterite road which could be difficult to negotiate in the wet season.

Sapele, Koko and Jakpa

a. Sapele

This is an old trading post and port on the confluence of the Ethiope and Jamieson rivers where they become the Benin River. The African Timber and Plywood Company (AT & P) is based here with a large sawmill and timber processing plant. The name 'Sapele' itself has been given to a type of hardwood exported from this region. The town of Sapele is not of great note except for some rather ornate old houses, but if you can hire a boat, a trip up the Jamieson River is a very pleasant outing. The AT & P Company, which is a subsidiary of the United Africa Company (UAC) has a guest house there, which can be used with their permission. If you cannot hire a boat, it is possible to get to the Jamieson River at Sapoba by car, where there is a pleasant picnic spot. The river upstream from Sapoba is beautifully clear, and suitable for swimming, although the water is surprisingly cold.

b. Koko

Koko received much publicity in 1988 owing to the dumping of toxic waste there. However, this has now been removed and the area is considered safe to visit. The traditional ruler has a palace in Koko, called the Nana's Palace.

c. Jakpa

This is an old trading post almost at the estuary of the Benin River which has an old canon, glass bottles and other relics of the past. The only way to reach it is to go by boat from Sapele down the Benin River. The banks of the river are covered in mangrove, very much a feature of the delta region of Nigeria.

Warri

Warri is one of the major oil ports of the delta region of Nigeria. It has a large refinery and an airfield. The old town is worth a visit if you are in Warri. There are many oil fields, oil pipelines and oil installations in the area. The area can easily be identified from the flaring of excess gas in huge jets of flame.

Route

From Benin City take the Sapele Road from the central roundabout and Warri is approximately 100 km to the south.

Hotels

The Palm Grove Motel, Upper Erejuwa Road, is adequate for an overnight stay.

to climb the inselberg should be obtained, and again a bottle of spirits may help. It is an energetic climb to the top, but a natural pool, curious depressions in the rock and the view are your rewards for the climb. From Lagos, approach via Abeokuta and take the Iseyin Road. It is approximately 40 minutes from Abeokuta.

e. Oke-Iho Village. It is a pleasant unspoilt African village due west of Iseyin.

f. Saki Town. This is an old city. May be worth seeing if you are going to Ogboro Inselberg and are making a day of it.

g. The Manor House. This is of interest to historians. It is on the top of the hill above the Catering Rest House in Iseyin. It was used by the British in colonial times as a residence and has superb views. The house was built on a grand scale with large rooms and an old fireplace. It is now used by the Oyo State Government.

Route

Iseyin is about 2 hours north-west of Ibadan and can be reached by going up the A1 Ibadan—Ilorin Road. In Oyo town, turn left (west) and approximately 40 km further on, you will come to Iseyin.

Hotels

There is a catering rest house, Trans-Nigeria Motels Ltd., on the Abeokuta road, which is adequate. The Nigerian Tobacco Company has a comfortable and fully-equipped Rest House, but it is only possible to use it if you have permission from the Managing Director in Lagos. Remember, however, that company rest houses are for the employees of the company, and it is a privilege to be allowed to use them. The NTC Rest House is just past the Trans-Nigeria Motel, on the right. It is best to bring your own provisions for the steward to prepare.

Jebba

General

Jebba is one of the crossing points over the River Niger. It is where the A1 main road and the railway to the north cross the river. Jebba has an important railway station and is of historical importance.

Tourist sites

a. The remains of Baikie's Boat, the 'Dayspring'. Baikie was sent to Africa to set up trading stations on the Niger but his boat unfortunately foundered on some hidden rocks at Jebba on October 7th, 1857. The only remaining relics of the boat are metal items, including the propeller, so it is of limited interest. They are at the railway station beside an old steam engine which would be of interest to children and railway buffs.

b. The Mungo Park and Lander monument, a white obelisk, is on the island in the middle of the river which is spanned by the bridges. To reach it, drive off the northbound bridge to the right by the police station, turn underneath the bridge to the left and park. Follow the path on foot across the railway line and up to the monument, where you will get a spectacular view. For further reading on Mungo Park, Lander and Baikie, see *The Story of the Niger River — The Strong Brown God* by Sanche de Gramont.

c. The Jebba Hydro-electric Dam—on the River Niger, north of Jebba. You can see it from the bridge; it is possible to visit it, with permission from NEPA.

d. Juju Rock. This is an outstanding rocky island in the

River Niger which can also be clearly seen from the bridge. It is here that some extraordinary Nupe bronze figures, dating from the 15th century, were discovered. The nine Toesede bronzes, from here and from the village of Tada, are the largest cast bronzes ever found in Africa, and six are now in the National Museum, Lagos. They have clear affinities with early Ife and Benin bronze-work.

Route

Lagos-Ibadan-Oyo-Ogbomoso-Ilorin bypass-Jebba. To take the Ilorin bypass, turn left (west) at a junction between Ogbomoso and Ilorin, signed to Jebba a few kilometres south of Ilorin.

Hotels

The National Paper Mills Guest House at Jebba is signed to the left just before the bridge, coming from the south. Follow the road up the hill to the guardpost of the paper mills compound and ask for directions. It is open everyday and provides a good basic lodging for the night. The view of the River Niger is superb at night.

Lake Kainji National Park, Borgu Sector

General

The Lake Kainji National Park consists of 2 separate parts: the Zurgurma Sector to the south-east in Niger State whose chalets, as at the time of writing, were still under construction, and the Borgu sector, west of Lake Kainji and the Dam, which already has accommodation for visitors.

Tourist sites

a. Kainji Dam. In 1958, Balfour Beatty, a British Company, was commissioned to look into the feasibility of a dam on the Niger. In 1964, the dam was started. The project was estimated to cost about £144 million, but ended up nearer £173 million. The dam itself was built by the Italians with British, Austrian, Swedish and Italian electrical equipment. There are 4 sections to the dam. The principal section is concrete, 5,486 m long with a height of 65.5 m. The generators were designed to produce 880 megawatts of power. Unfortunately, it has not succeeded in achieving this for many reasons, including lack of water. The artificial lake covers Old Bussa where Mungo Park, the explorer, was said to have come to grief in 1805. But the scene of the accident is no longer visible. The lake is 136 km long. Tours of the dam are available on request from the Nigeria Electric Power Authority (NEPA). Boat trips on the lake can be arranged by the Borgu Game Reserve office at Wawa. However, it is expensive unless there are several visitors to share the cost, and the road to the embarkation point is not good. Fishing is allowed on the lake.

b. Borgu Sector of Lake Kainji National Park. The park was set up as a Federal Game Reserve in 1979. It is 950 sq km and is one of the largest in West Africa. The area was uninhabited and the idea for the reserve was conceived in 1960. It is in the northern guinea vegetation zone which is characterised by tall grasses and savanna woodland. The reserve still has a reasonable animal population including antelope (kob), lion, hippopotamus, buffalo, roan antelope, jackal, baboon, monkey and crocodile but the elephants appear to have left the reserve. The reserve is open from December to June and the best time to visit is at the end of the dry season when the grass has died down and the animals have moved closer to the water. There is always the risk of harmattan from December to mid-February but this should not put you off.

3

South-east

Introduction

General

South-east Nigeria covers the area bordered by the River Niger in the west, the River Benue in the north, the border with Cameroon in the east and the Gulf of Guinea/Bight of Benin to the south. Much of the southern area consists of the delta region of the River Niger and its tributaries, with large areas of mangrove and swamps. In the east the country is mountainous and has the Oban Hills, and the Obudu and Mambilla Plateaux. Plateaux are features of this area, but the South-east also includes the Cross River

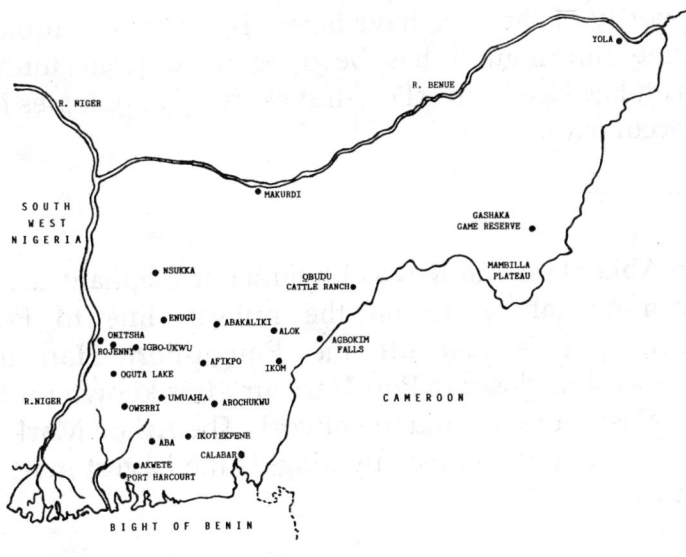

and the historical port of Calabar.

The South-east is the region of the oil industry which is of great economic importance to Nigeria. Between the River Niger and the Cross River valley there is an escarpment running north from Okigwe through Awgu and Udi to Nsukka and as far as the Benue valley, where some attractive hilly country can be seen.

This area has many different ethnic groups apart from the Igbo, the major group, whose culture dates back several centuries. It is very much the land of the masks, masquerades *(mmanwu)*, shrines and wood carvings, examples of which can be seen in the museums. The region has a strong Christian background as a result of the many missionaries who came to this part of the country from 1857 and founded a large number of schools. Festivals are very much a feature of this area, including the Christmas and New Year festivals held at most towns and villages. The New Yam Festivals are not held on the same day each year, so the dates must be checked locally.

Only the major tourist sites are covered, so it is always worth consulting the local people for further information. The majority of the sites have been visited by the author, but some information has been obtained from tourist guides and advice from fellow-travellers. My apologies for any inaccuracies.

Aba

Aba, in Abia State, (known as Enyimba or Elephant City), is a commercial centre on the railway line to Port Harcourt, and is just off the Enugu-Port Harcourt Expressway but closer to Port Harcourt. It is known for its textiles, glass, brewing and metalwork. The Ariara Market where you can buy almost anything, is the largest market in the area.

The main tourist site is the Museum of Colonial History, where the exhibits are almost entirely of old photographs and documents, which are very informative for anyone interested in Nigerian history. There is a craft centre in the museum grounds where they weave Akwete cloth, and it is possible to buy the cloth here, but of course, there is a better selection in the town of Akwete itself (*see* page 53). Aba was a garrison town and a District Headquarters in colonial times, and the museum is in an old colonial building on the outskirts of the town on the Ikot-Ekpene Road, A342. It is on the right of the road before crossing the Aba River bridge, and is worth a visit if you are passing that way. The museum is open from 9.00 a.m. to 6.00 p.m. daily.

Abakaliki

Abakaliki is in Enugu State, East of Enugu on the A343 Road to Ogoja, but at the time of writing the road was badly potholed. For those interested in Nigerian cloth, there is a good cloth market there, where local 'tie and dye' cloth, dyed in indigo, which is similar to Adire cloth, is sold.

Afikpo—Ishiagu Pottery

Afikpo is in the north-east corner of Imo State close to the Cross River, and is known for the pottery and mask making. On the Afikpo Road from Okigwe is the Afikpo Road Railway halt (station), and near here you can usually purchase Ishiagu pottery, on both sides of the Uturu-Afikpo road. Ishiagu itself is about 3 km away down a local road. The clay pots made in the area by the women are well designed and beautifully shaped, many decorated with figures and elaborate handles. Most of the pots have lids. Afikpo is also a traditional centre for mask making, which is done in the old central part of the town. Afikpo is an attractive hilly country, which is well worth a visit in its own right. For the nearest good accommodation, *see* Enugu (page 58).

Agbokim Waterfalls

Agbokim Waterfalls is a very attractive tourist spot near Ikom in Cross River State, close to the Cameroon border. It is an impressive sight, even in late December, so it would be magnificent in the wet season. It is less than 30 km from Ikom on a good tarred road, and would make an excellent picnic spot if you are travelling in the area, as you can drive right to the falls which are situated in pleasant forest surroundings. It is possible to climb down a rough path to the bottom of the valley where you can see underneath the overhang of the falls. There are no facilities at Agbokim, but Ikom has a motel overlooking the Cross River which is suitable for an overnight stop, called the Metro Hotel.

Route

From Ikom take the road towards the Cameroon border, but take the first turning left after about $1\frac{1}{2}$ km. Continue on this road for approximately 25 km, to the end of the road, through a village. The road ends in a circular roundabout' right beside the fall; so it is easy to find. The road is tarred and in good condition.

Agulu Lake

Agulu Lake is being developed as a tourist site. At present, it has the Idemili Cultural Centre and Rest House. It is 32 km south-east of Onitsha and may be worth a visit in the future if you are passing nearby.

Akwete Textile Centre

Akwete is a town in Abia State north-east of the Port Harcourt-Enugu Expressway. It is well-known for its brightly coloured cloth, which is woven by the women on a broad wooden loom about $1\frac{1}{2}$ m wide. The place is worth a visit if you are near Port Harcourt and interested in weaving. For accommodation, see page 72, on Port Harcourt.

Route

From Port Harcourt, take the expressway towards Enugu, and after about 45 km there is a turning to the right between a Texaco Petrol Station and an AP Petrol Station, where there is a sign pointing to the Akwete Rubber Research Institute (the sign is not very obvious). Continue along this winding road past the research institute, until you reach the village of Akwete. The weaving centre is in a new building on the right of the road, about 300 m past the large and well-built church.

Alok Stone Monoliths

There are a number of carved stone monoliths in Cross River State, but the best are around Alok, which is a small village about one hour north of Ikom on the Ogoja Road. The village is not marked. So the only way to find it is to ask along the road. It is on the left, some distance past an army camp which is 22 km from Ikom. The caretaker of the stones is most enthusiastic, and he will show you the monoliths in the village, (pictured in Peter Holmes's book, *Nigeria, Giant of Africa*), the sacred grove of 'cotton trees' just outside the village where sacrifices are made, and a circle of stones to the north of the village further along the main road. This latter area is controlled by the Department of Antiquities based at the National Museum in Lagos, where there are further examples of the monoliths on the lawn in front of the main building. The caretaker of the stones at Alok is SE Akong, who can be reached through Post Office Box 538, Ikom.

The sculptured granite stones represent human figures and are considered sacred by the local people. Their age is not known but the earliest may date from the 16th century. They represent an advanced form of stone-carving, as the granite is a hard crystalline rock, requiring a great deal of labour to produce such precise work. Other stones are to be found in the area, some in deep forest. Another site is in a grove at the roadside near Meghawe, a little beyond the mile 111 sign on the Enugu-Ogoja-Gboko Road. An annual festival is held there at the end of the dry season.

Hotels

There is a motel called the Metro at Ikom, overlooking the Cross River, to the south-west of the town, which is suitable for an overnight stop.

Arochukwu Shrine (The Long Juju)

The cave of the Oracle of the Long Juju is at Arochukwu in the south-east corner of Abia State, due south of Ohafia. The shrine is decorated with juju objects and has a long metal pipe through which the gods were said to speak. The Long Juju was said to have divine knowledge and was thought to know everything that was happening. A chief priest administered the shrine, assisted by agents who travelled far and wide in disguise, seeking out disputes. Once a dispute was encountered, the antagonists were persuaded to consult the Long Juju. The guilty party was thought to be devoured by the juju, but in reality it was a ruse as some were smuggled out of a back entrance and

Kalabari Masquerade, Bakana Island

Agbokim Falls near Ikom

The church at Akwete

Stone monoliths at Alok near Ikom

sold into slavery.

Although it was destroyed in the colonial days, it has been restored and the Long Juju is still respected by some of the local people. The nearest suitable accommodation is at Owerri or Port Harcourt (*see* pages 70 and 72). Unless you are especially interested in traditional religion, it is probably not worth a special visit, though it is of photographic interest, with permission.

Calabar

General

Calabar is well worth a visit, as it is an attractive city on the bank of the Calabar River near its junction with the Cross River and has a long history as the port of the eastern region of Nigeria, first visited by the Portuguese at the end of the 15th Century. It became the administrative headquarters of the Oil Rivers Protectorate, the British Protectorate of Southern Nigeria. (The oil in this case was palm oil, for which the region was an important trading centre). The history of Calabar is bound up with the history of the Efik ethnic group, of which the Obong of Calabar is the traditional ruler. The people trace their ancestry back to Babylon before the time of Christ. Calabar is also the centre from which many missionaries ventured forth in the 19th and 20th centuries, including Mary Slessor who arrived in Calabar in 1875. Her position was unique in this area. In spite of coming from the slums of Dundee in Scotland, she made such an impression that she became a Vice Consul at Okoyong, and the President of the Native Court. The Okoyong people called her 'The White Queen'.

Calabar is the capital of Cross River State and has good road and river communications into the hinterland. The town is served by an airport, linking it with Lagos and other parts of the country.

Tourist sites

a. The National Museum. This is in the old Residency building. The building was pre-fabricated and shipped from Britain and erected on the top of Consular Hill in 1884. The hill later became known as the Government Hill. The museum is well worth a visit just to see an old colonial building of such style on a site with superb views of Calabar and the Calabar River. The museum traces the history of Calabar and the surrounding area, and is extremely well set out. A guidebook is on sale, which is a valuable guide to the museum and a useful history book as well.

b. Mary Slessor's Cottage. This was at Ekenge across the river from Calabar, but the site is still commemorated by a cairn of stones. Mary Slessor's gravestone is in a graveyard in Enendem Street in Calabar, although it is rather neglected. It is on a hill at the south-west end of the town with a beautiful view over-looking the river. Her memorial, which was recently erected, is nearby.

Other Tourist Sites Outside Calabar

Oban Hills and Kwa Falls

This is a scenic area that is well worth seeing on a day-trip from Calabar. The falls are approximately 39 km from Calabar on the road towards Oban, at Aningeje, and you can drive right to the top of the falls where there is a bar, (not always open). The waterfall is in a deep valley with beautiful forest surroundings, and you can walk down the 150 or so steps to the river below. It is possible to walk upstream to the falls where there are deep pools, by scrambling over the rocks, but do remember to take insect repellent as the sandflies are vicious. Our climb down was rewarded by the sight of a giant kingfisher and a pair of mountain wagtails.

There are also tea plantations in this area and recently a Forest Reserve was opened. If you wish to visit this reserve, please contact a member of the Nigerian Conservation Foundation (NCF) in Lagos, 5, Moseley Road, Ikoyi, Tel: (01) 686163 or 687385.

Route

A direct route is Lagos-Benin City-Onitsha-Owerri-Aba-Ikot-Ekpene-Calabar. It is a two-day journey to Calabar but good stopping-off points would be either the Oguta Lake (*see* page 68) or the Concorde Hotel in Owerri, (*see* page 70). To get to the Oban Hills and Kwa Falls starting from the Metropolitan Hotel in Calabar, take the main dual carriageway north for about $2\frac{1}{2}$ km, then turn right at the traffic lights between the Mobil and National petrol stations onto the Oban Road. At the village of Aningeje, (about 34 km), go past the market and turn left at the sign which says 'Welcome to Palm Plantation Ltd, Kwa Falls Estate'. A laterite road leads through the oil palm estate for about 3 km to the falls. At a place where the road forks, there is a sign pointing right, in the direction of the falls.

Hotels

Calabar has no 5-star hotels, but the recommended hotel is the Metropolitan which is on the left of the dual carriageway as you enter Calabar. The telephone number is (087) 220911/2. An alternative is the Paradise Hotel at 86/88 Atekong Drive. Tel: (087) 225726. To get there, turn left off the dual carriageway down Atekong Drive, opposite the Ministry of Justice which can be seen on the right of the road just before reaching the Metropolitan Hotel.

Enugu

General

Enugu is the capital of Enugu State, one of the four Igbo States famed for the friendliness of its people and is the centre of the Nigerian coal industry, but do not let this put you off. It is situated in an attractive hilly country and is a well laid- out city with wide roads and expressways and main roads leading to the north, south, east and west. It is very much a centre of communications with an airport and the railway to Port Harcourt, passes through the city. It has some faculties of the University of Nigeria located in the city. It also boasts of one of the best hotels in Nigeria, as at the date of this guide (1991) the Nike Lake Hotel.

Tourist sites

The main places of interest are:
a. Enugu National Museum (closed in 1989 but to be re-opened and relocated on the Abakaliki Road).
b. Cultural Division Art Gallery, 7 Onitsha Road.

Route

The direct route is Lagos-Benin City-Onitsha-Enugu Expressway and takes about 7 hours. The expressway between Onitsha and Enugu was recently repaired and is, in good condition.

Hotels

The best hotel is the excellent Nike Lake Hotel which is to the north-east of Enugu. Travelling east on the dual carriageway you will see it signed to the left at the Penoks

Petrol Station, and it is well-signed from there on. It is a new hotel (built in 1988) in attractive surroundings with good management. There is a swimming pool and several tennis courts, and as the name implies, there is a small lake beside the hotel, with two rowing-boats for use by guests. Tel: (042) 337000. Telex 51448 NIKTEL EN ENG.

The other main hotel in Enugu is the Presidential, on Presidential Road, which has recently undergone a change of management. It is cheaper than the Nike Lake, but does not have the same facilities. Tel: (042) 337472.

Gashaka-Gumti Game Reserve

This is a vast expanse of spectacular wilderness, (6,000 km), in the south-east corner of Adamawa state, adjoining the Mambilla Plateau. Much of the reserve is mountainous, ranging from 457.2–2407 m, and Nigeria's highest mountain, Chapal Waddi (2,407 m) is in the reserve. It is the most ecologically diverse conservation area in the country and contains areas of guinea savanna, gallery forest, moist forest, and both montane forest and grassland. Many rivers flow through the reserve, including the Taraba, a major tributary of the River Benue. There is a wide variety of animal life including buffalo, hartebeest, roan antelope, chimpanzee, colobus monkey, hippopotamus, hyena, giant forest hog, lion and leopard. The reserve is a bird- watcher's paradise with a wide variety of species, and there is excellent fishing in the River Kam. The reserve headquarters is in the Forest Rest Houses at Serti, on the main road between Bali and the Mambilla Plateau. These rest houses provide self-catering accommodation at a small fee.

The entrance to the reserve is about 15 km south of Serti. In the dry season, it is possible to drive to the former headquarters at Gashaka village, some 30 km from the entrance gate, where more self-catering accommodation is available. The reserve is best explored on foot and it is possible to hire game guards, guides and porters at either Serti or in Gashaka village. Visitors planning to climb Chapal Waddi should collect a game guard from Serti and drive up to Njawai in the north-east corner of the plateau. Porters can be hired at Njawai and a 2-day trek is then needed to reach the top of the mountain.

Gashaka-Gumti is a most valuable resource, which has recently been neglected. It urgently deserves attention as it is one of the most important conservation areas in Nigeria.

For **Route and Hotels** *see* Mambilla Plateau on page 63.

Ikot-Ekpene

Ikot-Ekpene is in Akwa Ibom State. It is located on the road from Aba to Calabar but very close to Aba. It has an excellent tourist market on the left side of the road at Ikot-Ekpene junction. The variety of goods is first-class, with traditional musical instruments, handbags, wood carvings, masks and various other items of interest. Be prepared to bargain hard. A rule of thumb is to offer about a third of the price asked, and move upwards until you can reach an agreement.

Igbo-Ukwu

This is a small town, south-east of Onitsha. It was here that, by chance, in 1938, a man found some bronze artefacts while digging a well, but it was not until 1958 that the site was fully excavated by an English archaeologist, Thurstan Shaw, who revisited the site in 1989. The bronzes are dated to about the 9th century. Apart from this important discovery, the town has no other significance. Most of the bronzes are now in the

National Museum in Lagos, but when the author visited the village in 1989 there was a museum being built which will house the village chief's collection of artefacts.

Makurdi

General

Makurdi is the capital of Benue State, and it is here that the main A3 road bridge crosses the Benue River, beside the railway bridge. Makurdi is a good staging post en route north or south of the Benue River. There is a good new hotel there, and another under construction. The villages near Makurdi, south of the Benue, are interesting as they have a distinctive Tiv design, with a circular, open-sided meeting structure in the centre of the village. There is the Ikwe Holiday Resort, with chalets and a conference hall, approximately 20 km to the east of Makurdi along the Katsina Ala Road but turning into another road heading south. The resort is not yet fully-developed. For up-to-date information on this Holiday Resort, enquire at the Benue State Liaison Office in Victoria Island, Lagos.

Route

Since the new bridge across the Niger at Ajaokuta has been opened, the quickest route from Lagos to Makurdi is now via this bridge and thence to Ayangba, Ankpa, and the new road to Makurdi. At the time of writing, the road through Ankpa town was laterite, but all the rest of this route from the Niger is along good roads, and the journey can be done in 7 hours.

Hotels

The new Benue Hotel which is situated on a hill overlooking the Benue River, was opened in October 1989, and is to be recommended. The Makurdi Plaza is a slightly less-expensive alternative. Work on the new Sheraton Hotel, which was suspended, was due to begin again in 1990, and when completed it would be an excellent place to stay as it has a commanding position on a hill overlooking the Benue River.

All the 3 hotels are in the same area, and as a broad guide the hotels are all on the hill with the tall radio masts. At the main roundabout in the town, turn north and cross the railway line. Fork right off the dual carriageway where it curves to the left, and continue up the hill until you reach the Benue Hotel on the right, and the Sheraton a little further on. To get to the Makurdi Plaza, turn sharp right immediately after the right fork, and it is signed to the Hotel.

Mambilla Plateau

General

The Mambilla Plateau is in the south-east corner of Taraba State, which shares a border with the Cameroons. It is a high grassland plateau averaging over 1219 m, which is scenic, cool and a pleasant change from the heat and humidity of Lagos. It is recommended that visitors take all essentials, especially petrol, plenty of drinking water and possibly, camping equipment and food. There is no good hotel on the plateau, the roads are rough—to say the least—and the main town, Gembu, has few facilities. Power cuts are frequent and there are few telephones. However, it is a very attractive and interesting area and well worth a visit if you are well-prepared, as the area has cattle ranches, tea plantations and rolling grassy hills. It is very different from the rest of Nigeria in regard to flora and fauna, and is home to some rare species of birds and animals, especially at the Gashaka Game Reserve.

Kwa Falls, near Calabar

Ikot Ekpene tourist market

Obudu Cattle Ranch

The National War Museum, Umuahia

It is possible (but only in a 4-wheel drive vehicle) to drive into Cameroon from Gembu, across the Donga River via a 'punted' ferry and down a steep escarpment, but this is not for the faint-hearted or a vehicle with weak brakes. The route is normally only used by smugglers and intrepid travellers and it is essential to take advice before attempting it; we drove up the escarpment from the Cameroons in a Range Rover which tested the vehicle to the very limits.

Route

The best route to Mambilla is through Lagos-Benin City-Onitsha-Enugu-Otukpo-Yandev-Katsina Ala-Wukari-Mutum Biyu-Bali-Serti-Gembu, although an alternative is to cross the Niger by the new bridge at Ajaokuta, then go to Ankpa and thence to Otukpa and Otukpo, etc. In early 1990, the road from Enugu to Katsina Ala via Abakaliki had a very bad stretch and it was best to take the longer route via Otukpo and Yandev to Katsina Ala. The road via Takum and South Gida was also very bad in early 1989. So, again it is advisable to take the alternative route via Wukari. Do not be tempted to take the short-cut from Yandev to Mbatie and Zaki Biam. As at 1989 there was no ferry over the Katsina Ala River. There is an alternative route onto the plateau via Baissa, but part of this was washed away in March 1989 and it may take a long time to repair, so do not attempt this route without checking first.

Hotels

There is a basic Government Guest House in Gembu which can be booked through the Taraba State Liaison Office in Lagos, and a simple hotel called The Daula. It is also possible, with permission, to stay at the tea plantation owned by the Nigerian Beverage Production Company. They have no office in Lagos, but their headquarters is at

Yola, next to the airport, and a request for accommodation could be sent to them by courier service, but this is a privilege, not a right. The Upper Benue River Basin Authority also have a Guest House, near the Gembu airstrip, in the old Forestry Department Guest House. Again, permission must be obtained first. Permission and directions can be obtained from the Department of Wildlife & Forestry in Serti.

Nsukka

Nsukka is in the north of Enugu State, due north of Enugu. Its claim to fame is that it hosts the University of Nigeria, which is the oldest indigenous university, all the older ones having been set up before independence and affiliated with universities in England. Within the campus of the university is an excellent museum which contains stone-age relics, old pottery, traditional masks and many other interesting items connected with the area. If you are passing, or staying at Enugu, this museum is well worth a visit. It is well-laid out, has many fascinating exhibits and is not too large. Just north of the turning to Nsukka is a village with a lorry park, called Obollo-Afor. Here you can buy brightly coloured baskets (from the roadside stalls) of a type not seen elsewhere in Nigeria.

Obudu Cattle Ranch

General

The Obudu Cattle Ranch is a popular tourist site in the north-east corner of Cross River State, close to the Cameroonian border. The Obudu Plateau is over 1,524 m and the climate is cool and very pleasant. The landscape is spectacular with rolling grassland, deep-wooded valleys and waterfalls. It is best to visit Obudu in the dry season, in the rainy season much of the ranch may be covered in mist and low cloud and there are spectacular thunder storms. Sometimes between December and February the harmattan is heavy. So the best times are the end of October to December and March and April.

Tourist sites

The major attractions of the Obudu Cattle Ranch are:

a. The Waterfall—approximately 3 hours hard walking each way. In spite of the altitude it can get very hot in the daytime so carry plenty of water, as the walk is mostly along the tops of the grass-covered ridges. It is best to take a guide, who will lead you to the top of the waterfall where there is a shady place for a picnic. The best view of the waterfall is from across the valley, not far from the ranch.

b. Natural Swimming Pool or 'grotto'. This is only a short walk from the Ranch House and is in a pleasant shady setting. It is large enough for a quick dip but no more.

c. The Gorilla Camp is approximately 13 km from the hotel. So, it is a very long day's trek, (approximately 8 hours for the round trip). In 1988, it was proved that there were gorillas on the Obudu Plateau, but it is doubtful whether visitors would be lucky enough to see them, as they are very shy animals.

d. Horse riding is ₦10 per hour, and there are only a limited number of saddles.

e. Bird watching—there are many unusual species of birds at Obudu, owing to its montane habitat; so take your binoculars and field guide.

f. Sports facilities—tennis court, squash court, crazy-golf course (putting only).

g. Walking—there are many interesting walks, so take good walking shoes, and a small backpack for water, etc, and it is probably best to engage a guide. One of the best walks is along the track from the farm to the cataract, near the border with Cameroon.

It is wise to book the chalets beforehand as the hotel can be full at peak times like public holidays and weekends, and it can be done in one of the following ways:

a. Through the Cross River State Liaison Office, Victoria Island, Lagos (near Bar Beach).

b. Write to the Obudu Cattle Ranching Co. Ltd., P.O. Box 37, Obudu, Cross River State.

c. Radio through to the Ranch from the Obudu Local Government Office, in Obudu town.

d. Obudu Cattle Ranch Office, No. 2 Barracks Road, ADC Building, Calabar.

Route

The direct route is through Lagos-Benin City-Enugu-Abakaliki-Ogoja; turn right to Vandeikya and Obudu town (the turning is unsigned). However, the Abakaliki Road was in very bad condition as at the time of writing and we were advised to go via Otukpa-Otukpo-Yandev-Katsina Ala and then turn left off the Ogoja Road towards Vandeikya. It was a longer route but as our informant said it had taken him 3 or 4 hours to travel 100 km on the Abakaliki route, it was obviously the wiser choice. If it is possible, take up-to-date advice on the state of these roads. In Obudu turn left at a T-junction near the Post Office and follow the road towards Ikom. Approximately 4 km from Obudu, the cattle ranch is signed to the left, and from there it is approximately another 60 km to the ranch. Once you reach the ranch entrance at the bottom of the plateau you begin to climb very steeply for the last 11 km. There are 20 hairpin bends so make sure your brakes are in good condition! The road surface is good but, of course, the gradient is very steep. It is at least a 12-hour journey from Lagos, and it is better to break the journey at Enugu where the recommended hotel is the Nike Lake Hotel (*see* section on Enugu, page 58). If you are visiting Calabar, the route is via Ikom, and will take you up to 5 hours.

Hotels

The ranch has a hotel with chalets. The accommodation consists of:

a.   11 VIP chalets (4 rooms in each)
b.   6 suites
c.   16 single rooms

The hotel has a dining room which is not expensive and serves basic food, normally with a set menu and no choice. It is advisable to take some of your own food for picnics, etc.

Ogbunike Cave

This cave is just south of the Onitsha-Enugu Expressway, a few kilometres from Onitsha. It has not been developed as a tourist site, as it is a shrine for the local people, so you must gain permission from a guide at St Monica's Secondary School nearby before entering it, and then negotiate a good price for the guide's services. The cave is in a small valley and there is a large entrance to the first cave, but it is possible to crawl through a tunnel for a hundred metres or so, and emerge further down the valley. There are small bats roosting in one of the tunnels and strange spiders and insects can be seen by shining a torch onto the roof of the main cave. Children who like 'spooky' experiences would enjoy this cave, but wear old clothes and take a torch. It is essential to take a guide.

Route

The cave is near the village of Ogbunike on the Onitsha-Awka (pronounced Oka) Road. From the direction of Onitsha, when you reach Ogbunike look for a sign on the left of the road printed 'St Monica's Secondary School'. Follow this road (potholed) for about 2 km until you reach the school. Ask for a guide, who will then unlock the barrier and you can drive another kilometre on a dirt track to the parking place above the cave.

Oguta Lake Resort

General

The Oguta Lake Resort has a motel near the lake, an 18-hole golf course, a tennis court and table-tennis. There is also a children's playground and an old Civil War Bunker, (the 'Ojukwu Bunker'), which is close to the Club House on the golf course. The motel is set in peaceful surroundings with pleasant walks, and the staff are friendly and helpful.

The motel has about 60 rooms made up of presidential suites and double rooms. The golf course is not up to European championship standards but is satisfactory. The village of Oguta on the other side of the lake can be reached by car-ferry or canoe, and it is possible to hire a motor boat for excursions. If you are in the area, Oguta is worth a visit as an alternative to staying at Owerri. Regattas are sometimes held on the lake.

Route

The Oguta Lake Resort is north-west of Owerri, the capital of Imo State and the town of Oguta is marked on most road maps. The route is Lagos-Benin City-Onitsha — turn south towards Owerri — turn right (west) at Mgbidi and when you get to Oguta town, ask for directions to the car-ferry. The ferry runs every 20 minutes or so across the kilometre wide lake, and can take several cars. From the landing stage, it is only $\frac{1}{2}$ km to the motel. If you are approaching from Owerri there is no need to take a ferry. Turn left off the main Owerri-Onitsha Road at Ogbaku, and continue along the road until you reach a T-junction. Turn right and you will soon reach the motel opposite the golf course.

Onitsha

Onitsha is on one of the major bridge crossings over the River Niger, in Anambra State. It has always been an important commercial city, showing great enterprise and entrepreneurial skills. The main market in Onitsha is said to be the largest and best-stocked in West Africa. To see it all takes the best part of a day. Most travellers pass through Onitsha on their way to Enugu and places east. Onitsha has no modern hotels and the only hotel that has been mentioned by a fellow traveller is the Niger Heritage Regency Hotel, 1 Heritage Drive, Omagba Layout, P.O. Box 3850, which is said to be satisfactory. Some of the roads in the town are badly affected by water erosion, which can seriously delay traffic.

Oron

Oron is in the south-east corner of Akwa-Ibom State, on the Cross River, and is worth visiting for its National Museum. The museum, which overlooks the river, is next to the embarkation point for the Calabar car-ferry. The museum is mainly about the local Oron people and has an important collection of wooden Ekpu memorial carvings, which portray the male ancestors of the Ibibio people. They are believed to be between 2 and 3 centuries old. The importance of the Oron carvings was first recognised when Kenneth C Murray, then an Art master at the Teachers' Training College, Uyo, observed them in 1938. Unfortunately, many of the Ekpu carvings were destroyed in the civil war, but there is a well-preserved Civil War Bunker, as this was an important defensive point overlooking the river.

The ferry to Calabar goes once a day and takes 2 hours, but does not run at very regular times. Oron is about an hour's drive from Uyo, the state capital, but shortly before reaching the town there were several kilometres of laterite road as at 1990. There is the Metropolitan Hotel in Uyo near the State House, which is adequate. There are plans to build a new hotel in Uyo soon.

Owerri

Owerri is the capital of Imo State. Imo is mostly a one-ethnic group state inhabited by the Igbo people. The Igbos are renowned for their music and dancing, especially their masquerades when the dancers wear elaborate masks. Owerri itself is dominated by the Assumpta Catholic Cathedral which towers above all other buildings in the centre of the town and is one of the cleanest and best laid-out cities in Nigeria. The only places of interest to visit are the Mbari Cultural Centre and Museum, and the Zoological Garden, Nekede, on the outskirts of the town.

Route
Lagos-Benin City-Onitsha-Owerri.

Hotels
The Imo Concorde Hotel is one of the more modern hotels in the country, with a large swimming pool, and is definitely to be recommended. Alternatively, you can stay

P.O. BOX 816 KATSINA
TEL: (065) 31165-9

MEMBER OF
MURADI MOTEL'S LIMITED

LIYAFA PALACE HOTEL KATSINA

Home of Hospitality and Excellence

AN OASIS IN THE DESERT

A hotel of international standard that offers you fully air-conditioned rooms with satellite dish for cable television,

mini-bar, conference centre, banquet hall and also swimming pool, tennis court facilities for our guests.

MURTALA MUHAMMED MEMORIAL BOTANICAL GARDENS

* Picnic Gardens
* Plant Nursery
* Research Centre
* Library
* Floral Museum
* Catering Complex
* Swimming Pool
* Guided Tours
* Bridal Garden
(for wedding & Wedding Reception)

Visit our Floral Centre at Osborne Road Shopping Complex Ikoyi for your fresh flowers; flower pot and vases, plant food and medicaments; garderning tools Consultancy on landscape designs etc.

Okorisan, Abomiti Junction, Klm. 6 to Epe, Maroko - Epe Expressway, Lagos.
Shop 4, Tafawa Balewa Square, Lagos, Tel: 623413, 688474

at the Oguta Lake Motel, (*see* page 68), which is within an hour from Owerri.

Port Harcourt

General

Port Harcourt is the capital of Rivers State and is the centre of the oil industry in Nigeria. It is called 'The Garden City' as it has many more trees and parks than most cities in Nigeria. Port Harcourt is now the second most important port in Nigeria although it did not exist before 1913. Nearby are the 2 historical ports of Bonny and Brass, which were formerly connected with the slave trade, but are now better known as oil ports and terminals.

Tourist sites

a. The Rivers State Museum. The museum is presently housed in the Secretariat buildings, although there are plans to move it to a specially-designed building. The museum has many examples of local culture, especially masks and carvings, and it is worth a visit.

b. Rivers State Cultural Centre. The State Cultural Centre is in Bonny Street which is down in the old part of the town, and has a stage and auditorium for plays and dancing and a shop where you can purchase local handicrafts.

c. Boat trips. Port Harcourt is at the head of the delta area and it is possible to take a boat trip down the creeks of the delta to Bonny. You will pass through mangrove swamps and see the many fishing villages along the shores of the creeks. If you go ashore at Bonny be sure to take an identity card as the immigration department may require proof of identity. Also, it is advisable not to photograph any of the oil installations. Bonny has an exciting festival with war canoes on Christmas Day and Opobo has a similar festival on New Year's Day.

d. Golf Course. There is a very pleasant and well-groomed golf course at Port Harcourt. It has recently been increased to 18 holes, and is one of the best courses in Nigeria.

e. Azumini Blue River. This is an attractive picnic place about an hour's drive from Port Harcourt between Akwete and Azumini. The river has beautiful clear blue water with sandy beaches. It is possible to hire a canoe to take you for a short journey along the river to one of the clean, sandy beaches where there are wooden chairs, tables and a BBQ grill provided for picnics. From Port Harcourt take the Enugu Expressway for about 45 km until you reach a turning to the right between a Texaco and an AP petrol station. Continue through the village of Akwete (see page 53), until you reach the bridge over the river near Azumini. You can hire canoes from near the bridge to take you to the beaches.

Route

To get to Port Harcourt, the following route is suggested. Lagos-Benin City-Sapele-Warri roundabout-Patani-Ahoada-Port Harcourt. The road between the turn-off to Warri and the bridge at Patani was repaired in early 1990 and is now a good road. This route takes between 6 and 7 hours.

Hotels

The Presidential Hotel is the main hotel in Port Harcourt with a large swimming pool and two good restaurants; a Lebanese restaurant called the Why Not and a Chinese Restaurant, both serving excellent food. It receives satellite TV from Europe and America and is considered a good hotel. It can be seen on the right as you are entering Port

Harcourt on the dual carriageway. Take the slip road right, shortly before the hotel, Tel: (084) 300260-2 Telex: 61308, PMB 5141.

There is another hotel called the Olympia, 45 Force Road, near the golf course which is in the main residential area. The location is pleasant but the service is slow.

There is also the Airport Hotel at the International Airport which is about 30 minutes drive from the city. It is a good alternative to the hotels in the city, especially if you are travelling by air. Tel: (084) 310400-13 and 334721.

Rojenny Tourist Village

This tourist village, which is just outside Onitsha at the kilometre 11 mark on the Onitsha-Owerri Road, was still under construction as at late 1989. Once completed it should have accommodation, a restaurant, a miniature zoo, tennis courts, swimming pool, dance hall, amusement park, joy-rides and various other attractions, including a make-believe 'shrine'. The tourist village is the brain-child of Chief RA Ezeonwuka and was started in November 1986.

Umuahia National War Museum

The National War Museum is located at Ebite Amafor Isingwu on the outskirts of Umuahia, which is due east of Owerri, capital of Imo State and close to the Enugu-Port Harcourt Expressway. The museum is extremely well-laid out, very interesting and informative and a 'must' if you are in the area of Owerri or Port Harcourt. Apart from exhibitions of war relics from pre-colonial times, there are displays of the Enugu coal miners' riot, the Aba women's riot, Tiv riots, Niger Delta and Maitatsine (Kano) religious disturbances. There is an excellent section with photographs, maps and exhibits of the Nigerian Civil War.

The radio room used by the Biafrans during the war is on display, as well as tanks, aircraft, boats and weapons. Umuahia is the capital of Abia state, created in 1991.

Yola

General

Yola is the capital of Adamawa State, on the upper reaches of the Benue River and is close to some of the most scenic areas of Nigeria which lie along the mountainous border with Cameroon. Yola has no tourist sites itself, but it does have a fishing festival in April and is a base for touring in the area. The very scenic Mandara mountains north of Yola, (pictured in Peter Holmes's book, *Nigeria, Giant of Africa*) are described on page 118 of this book, but are well within reach of Yola. The Mambilla Plateau described on page 62 is within a day's journey from Yola as are the Shebshi mountains to the south.

Route

From Lagos there are several routes to Yola. One is via Benin-City-Onitsha-Enugu-Otukpo-Yandev-Katsina Ala-Wukari-Jalingo-Numan-Yola, or cross the Niger via the new bridge at Ajaokuta, and from there to Ankpa, south to Otukpa and thence to Otukpo, etc. The road from Enugu via Abakaliki was very rough in early 1990, so do not go this way without taking up-to-date advice. The road between Wukari and Numan was badly potholed in places in 1990. So, unless the road has been improved, allow extra time for your journey. There is an alternative route after Jalingo via Zing and Mayo Belwa, but the answer is to seek advice from the local taxi drivers as to the state of these roads. From Abuja, the route is through Jos-Bauchi-Gombe-Numan-Yola.

Hotels

A new luxury hotel called the International Hotel was opened in early 1990, and is the recommended hotel in Yola, but there are several less expensive hotels including the Taraba Hotel on Secretariat Road, the Peacock Hotel on Mubi Road and the Hamco on Airport Road which are all adequate for an overnight stop. The International Hotel is on Kashim Ibrahim Road, Tel: (075) 25739 or 25459.

4
North-west

Introduction

General

North-west Nigeria covers the area bordered by the River Niger to the south and west, the Niger Republic to the north, and the state boundaries of Kano, Kaduna, and Abuja, the Federal Capital Territory, to the east. Thus, the area includes the states of Niger, Sokoto, Katsina, Kano, Kaduna, Kebbi and the F.C.T.

This region does not have as many tourist sites as the south of the country, but it is a very interesting area to visit, with an entirely different historical background, as traditionally it has looked north across the Sahara for its trade, rather than south to the sea. The vegetation, climate, terrain and people are also markedly different from those in the south. For this reason alone a visit to the north is a 'must' for those living in Lagos or in any of the other cities of the south.

North-west Nigeria is fascinating for its strong Hausa/Fulani traditions, walled cities, and great Sallah festivals, with its spectacular durbars. *Id-el-Fitri* marks the end of the Muslim period of Ramadan; *Id-el-Kabir* is a Muslim thanksgiving ceremony commemorating the substitution of Isaac with the sacrificial ram, and *Id-el-Maulud* marks the Prophet Muhammed's birthday. The internationally renowned Argungu Fishing Festival is another colourful event which is one of the great festivals of Nigeria. The landscape, which borders on the desert to the north, is studded with extraordinary inselbergs rising out of the surrounding countryside like great stone altars. In fact, many of these have strong religious significance to the local people and therefore permission should be sought before climbing them. The most astounding is Zuma Rock on the Lokoja-Kaduna Road, shortly after passing the turn-off to Abuja. It is a huge mass of sheer granite towering above the landscape, streaked with vertical lines and with the apparent likeness of a face etched into its southern side.

The crafts and culture of the north are also very different from the south, especially the leather work in Sokoto, the indigo dye-pits in Kano, and the glass and metalwork in Bida. Also, there is a great variety of beautiful pottery, which can often be bought by the side of the road.

Most of the places described have been visited by me recently, nevertheless changes are always taking place, tourism is on the move in Nigeria and my information may soon be dated. Although the site will remain, the tourist infrastructure around it may change. So please bear with me if some of the facts are not up to date.

Abuja

General

Abuja needs little introduction. It is the new capital of Nigeria whose four phases of development will probably extend well into the next century. The first phase saw the main government buildings constructed, including government secretariats, the presidential palace and guest houses, libraries, museums, parks, parade grounds, local government buildings, diplomatic missions and their accompanying residences. New roads, powerlines, water, sewage systems and telephone lines have been constructed while other projects are being executed. Three hotels have already been completed: the excellent Nicon-Noga Hilton managed by the British Hilton Hotels, (part of Ladbrokes of the United Kingdom), the Sheraton Hotel, which opened in early 1990 and the Agura. A fourth hotel is planned. One of the outstanding features of this new city is the large golden domed mosque which dominates the town. It was completed in 1990.

Tourist sites

a. The plant nursery and reservoir below the Abuja inselberg.

b. Usuma dam and reservoir off the northern dual carriageway, about 40 minutes from Abuja. Consult the hotel management about gaining permission to enter the dam. A pleasant picnic spot.

SPECTRUM ROAD MAP OF NIGERIA

In an expanding country like Nigeria, where growth is constant, it is vital to have the most up-to-date maps available. The new Spectrum Road Map of Nigeria is fully revised, clear and comprehensive. International and state boundaries, expressways, roads and tracks are included, along with all communications i.e. railways, major and minor airports, rivers and ferries. There is useful information on local landscape types -swamps and areas likely to flood. Full contour colouring allows the lie of the land to be judged at a glance. For short journeys or long treks - the Spectrum Road Map of Nigeria is an invaluable companion.

Size: 762 × 1016mm (30'' × 40'') Flat
255 × 140mm (10'' × 5½'') Folded
Scale: 1:1 500 000

Available from airports and leading bookshops, or in case of difficulty from:
Spectrum Books Ltd. Sunshine House,
1, Emmanuel Alayande Street, Oluyole Industrial Estate,
P.M.B. 5612, Ibadan.
Telex: 31588   Telephone: 310058-311215-310145

c. Zuma Rock—*see* page 103
d. The IBB International Golf and Country Club is virtually completed. The Phase I (First Nine Holes) is ready for use.
e. Pottery market on the Lokoja-Kaduna Road just before the first Abuja turn-off if you are coming from the south. A large selection of Gwari pots, jugs and bowls are on sale here. They are not expensive and are beautifully designed.
f. Gurara Falls on the Minna road—*see* page 88.
g. Dr Ladi Kwali's pottery at Suleja—*see* page 101.

Route

There are several ways of travelling to Abuja by road from Lagos. The best route is Lagos-Benin Expressway-Ore-Ondo-Akure-Owo-Ipele-Kabba-Lokoja-Abuja.
Alternatively you can go via Benin City and Auchi, or via Ibadan-Jebba-Bida and Abuja. It takes between 8 and 10 hours depending on your route.

Hotels

The Nicon-Noga Hilton is of international standard and is one of the very best in Nigeria. It is expensive, but there are special 'Royal Weekends' with reduced rates. It has every facility including a large swimming pool, tennis courts, squash courts, gymnasium, sauna and night club. Tel. (09) 5231811–830. Telex 71504 HILTON NG.

The Sheraton Towers Hotel opened in early 1990, also provides all the facilities of an international hotel. Tel. (09) 5230225–244. Telex (09) 91520.

The smaller Agura Hotel is on Festival Road. It has a swimming pool, tennis courts and a night club, and is a comfortable hotel. Tel. (09) 2341753–760. Telex: 71496 AGURA NG.

Argungu

General

Argungu is famous for its fishing festival normally held on a Saturday near the end of February/early March, but the date very much depends upon when the state government and the Emir of Argungu decide to hold it. Enquiries can be made from the Kebbi State Liaison Office, 17 Adeola Odeku St., Victoria Island, Lagos. The festival lasts for 4 days, the climax being the fishing competition, but many other activities take place during the period: archery, cultural dancing, camel and donkey racing, bicycle racing, wrestling, boxing (Nigerian style) and agricultural show, handicraft exhibition and the Kabanci display (water events) at the area called Mala. The main reason for tourists to go to Argungu is to see the fishing festival. Its origins are said to date back to the 16th century when the great Mohammed Kanta, founder of the Kebbi empire, held a festival to mark the end of the fishing season. The modern form dates back to 1934. The festival takes place at a site called the Matan Fada where a large pavilion has been built on the side of the Rima River. The present Emir, His Royal Highness, Alhaji Muhammadu Mera is a descendant of King Kanta and has his palace in Argungu. Most of the local people are Kabawa.

Procedure for the fishing festival

Thousands of fishermen, each carrying a large gourd and 2 hand nets resembling the wings of a huge butterfly, form up in line about 500 m from the river. On a signal from the Emir, a gun is fired and the fishermen race towards the river in a sensational, mile-long charge. They pour into the river in front of the stands until it becomes a seething mass of bodies, nets and gourds, creating a magnificent sight. Judges, officials and musicians in boats steer their way in amongst the crowds of fishermen, adding to the colourful scene. The fishermen who catch the largest fish are escorted to the centre of the pavilion where their catch is weighed and both the fish and fisherman are tagged for future reference. About 2 hours after the start, another gun signals the end of the contest. Then the fish are graded according to weight and a substantial prize is given to the man who has caught the largest fish, with smaller prizes for the runners-up. The winning fish is normally between 32 and 98 kg. Fishing is then forbidden in this part of the river until the festival in the following year.

It pays to get to the stands early, at about 8.00 am, to get a seat. The Governor and the official party arrive around 9.30 am and the fishing competition begins at 10.00 am. It is all over by about 1.00 p.m.

In summary, this festival is well worth a visit even if you can only spare the time for the final day. There is also a small museum in Argungu, in the old palace of the Emir, built in 1849, called the Kanta Museum, which is of interest as it gives an insight into the local history, culture and weaponry, including an example of the horse-armour once used in local battles, and a suit of chain mail. It has objects which are up to 500 years old, including those which belonged to Mohammed Kanta, 1516-1554, the founder of the Kebbi Empire. The villages around Argungu are also of special interest as they have attractive round granaries. In March, near the end of the dry season, the area is very arid, and camels are a familiar sight.

Route

The best route to Argungu is Lagos-Ibadan-Ilorin (or the Ilorin by-pass)-Jebba-Kontagora-Yelwa-Jega—then take the Sokoto

Road until the turn-off to Argungu about 20 km past Shagari, although there is an alternative, but untried, route from Jega through Kalgo and Birnin Kebbi. It is a good two-day journey by car, and after Ilorin the route is not blessed with good hotels. An alternative is to go via Abuja, but it is 2 days hard driving. Flying to Sokoto is another option, but of course, the planes will be heavily booked at the time of the festival.

Hotels

Booking for the fishing festival and reservations at the 60 room Grand Fishing Hotel must be made at least one month beforehand, through the Kebbi State Liaison Office, 17 Adeola Odeku St., Victoria Island, Lagos. On arrival in Argungu, the Fishing Hotel is very obvious as it is on the left as you enter the town. If you cannot book accommodation there, try Sokoto which is about one hour's drive away on a reasonable road—*see* page 101 on Sokoto, for hotels. Grand Fishing Hotel PMB 1411 Argungu, Kebbi State. Tel. (060) 550547, 550543, 550544 or 550546.

Bagauda Lake Hotel, Tiga Dam

General

The Bagauda Lake Hotel has been developed as a conference centre with chalets, a swimming pool and nightclub, and is some 56 km south of Kano. Further along the road is the Rock Castle Hotel, overlooking the Tiga Dam and reservoir. It is in an attractive environment, but unfortunately, the hotel is under-used. It is a pleasant spot for anyone wanting to get away from the rush and bustle of Kano, but is really too far from the city for a convenient overnight stop. Tiga Dam is a pleasant picnic spot not too far from Kano.

Route

From Kano take the Zaria Road towards the south, and after about 50 km there is a major turning on the left which is marked 'Bagauda Lake Hotel'. The hotel is reached after a few kilometres. The Tiga Dam and Rock Castle Hotel are approximately 24 km further down this road.

Bida

General

Bida is a fascinating town, renowned for its handicrafts, its colourful market and the fact that it is the main city of the Nupe tribe. The Emir or Etsu Nupe, has a palace in the town. Bida is famous for its glass beads, cloth, silver and brasswork, its carved 8-legged stools made from a single piece of wood, and for its decorative pottery, although the latter is only found in villages nearby.

The market, which is in the centre of the old town, soon to be modernised, is one of the most colourful traditional markets in Nigeria. The silver and brasswork may be seen on either side of the main road leading from the first town gate, (if you are coming from the west), towards the market. The beadmakers and some brassworkers are in Musaga Road, which is on the right, off the Bida bypass when you are heading towards Lapai. The turn-off is almost opposite the Lafiya Clinic which you can see on the left of the road. The beadmakers, whose raw materials are melted beer bottles and coloured glass jars, are about 400m on the left and the brassworkers a little further up the road, on the right. If you agree to offer them some 'dash', the craftsmen will allow you to watch them make their beads and bangles, using an earthenware kiln and handmade bellows. Some interesting pottery can be bought near the Kaduna River bridge on the Bida side. Nearby villages have similar pottery for sale as well as the

8-legged Bida stools.

Route

From Lagos you go through Ibadan-Ilorin (or Ilorin by-pass)-Jebba, — turn right just after Mokwa-Bida. You arrive on the Bida bypass which skirts the north of the town. The old town is to your right through the gates, but see directions above to the beadmakers. The journey takes between 7 and 8 hours from Lagos.

From Abuja, take the northern dual-carriageway out of the city onto the Kaduna Road. Turn left towards Suleja and Minna shortly after passing Zuma Rock. Turn left (south-west) at Lambatta, through Lapai to Bida.

Hotels

Unfortunately, there are no good hotels in Bida, though there is a Catering Rest House in the Government Residential Area. An alternative is to make it a day's outing from Abuja or Minna. *See* pages 79 and 99 for hotels in these towns.

Birnin Gwari

General

Birnin Gwari has a wildlife reserve called Kamuku. It has some of the larger game animals, and monkeys, baboons, warthog, etc. It is also excellent for bird-watching. You may see the rare ground hornbill, which is almost the size of a turkey, in the area. The reserve is not as well-known or as well-preserved as the main reserves in Nigeria, but could make an interesting stop, although there is only basic accommodation. If you are in the area, the Dogon Ruwa River is also worth a visit, especially for bird-watchers. The end of the dry season is the best time to visit. Please note that there are *two* Birnin Gwari in

Kaduna State shown on the map, but the Game Reserve is the one near the village due west of Kaduna: the southern Birnin Gwari. Kaduna State has plans to develop this Game Reserve further.

Route

Kaduna is the best base for visiting the reserve. Take the Lagos Road from Kaduna to Birnin Gwari, and after the village there is a turning to the left. The Wildlife Officer's bungalow is down this road on the left. The reserve itself is approximately 1 km further down the Lagos Road, but to the right of the road. The chalets overlooking the lake, beside the main road in Birnin Gwari, provide very basic accommodation, but there is no restaurant.

To get to the Dogon Ruwa River, drive to Birnin Gwari from the Kaduna direction, and in the middle of the village there is a junction just after the water tower. Turn right (Funtua Road) and proceed for 11 km until you reach a construction camp and quarry. The hamlet just after that is Kungi and at the end of the village is a track to the left. Follow this track for 3 km until you come to a waterfall and from there you can walk along the river.

Birnin Kebbi

Birnin Kebbi is an old traditional Hausa walled town which has recently become the capital of Kebbi state, created in 1991. It is south-west of Argungu, and makes an interesting stop if you are touring the north-west, or visiting the Argungu Fishing Festival.

Birnin Kudu

Birnin Kudu is known for its rock paintings, similar to those found in the Sahara. The paintings which are dated at 800–850 years ago are of cattle and wild animals, but the ones we saw were small and not very clear, and the protective cage around them rather detracted from their effect. There are paintings on both sides of the main road. Those on the left are the clearer. It is necessary to get a guide to show you the paintings when you reach Birnin Kudu, which is south-east of Kano on the A237 Road to Maiduguri. There is no good hotel in the area, so it is only worth visiting if you are passing through Birnin Kudu. The nearest base for visiting this area is either Kano or Bauchi..

Chafe

Chafe is mentioned only because of its market which is held on a Sunday. It is 128 km from Zaria on the Sokoto Road between Funtua and Gusau. It is a traditional Fulani market and apart from the interesting variety of livestock, both leather workers and calabash carvers can be seen at work. Fulani hats and their decorative rugs are also on sale. Also, many Fulani come to the market in their traditional dress which makes it a colourful sight. You may chance upon a Fulani bride-choosing ceremony or their manhood-proving contests when the young men beat each other with sticks, and vie to become 'the bravest of the brave'. We have witnessed both in our travels, although neither was in Chafe. The Fulani do not seem to mind being photographed; it enhances their reputation for good looks, but it is always better to ask first. Like many of the other fascinating markets in the north, it is well worth a visit if you are passing through Chafe on a Sunday.

Daura

General

Daura is a historical town owing to its position as the spiritual home of the Hausa. With Katsina, it was an

Abuja Mosque at night

Gwari village near Abuja

Argungu Fishing Festival

Nupe craftsmen, Bida

important trading town, but it has since declined owing to changes in the trading patterns in the north of Nigeria. There are various legends about the origins of the Hausa kingdoms. The most popular is the legend that Bayajidda Abuyazidu, son of Abdulahi, King of Baghdad, left home after a quarrel with his father in 900 AD. He came to Daura via the Kingdom of Borno, where he married the daughter of the Mai of Borno. He was later forced to flee because the Mai was jealous of him. He took his wife and concubine, Gwari, with him.

On arriving at Daura he asked for a drink, but was informed that a snake called Sarki, which lived in the well, only allowed water to be drawn on a Friday. Bayajidda was not having this, so he went to the well to draw water. The snake rose up to strike the intruder but Bayajidda struck off the snake's head with his sword. The Queen of Daura was deeply impressed and married Bayajidda for his bravery. They had a son called Bawo, who in turn had six sons who later became the rulers of Daura, Kano, Rano, Katsina, Zaria and Gobir.

These six states, together with Biram ruled by Bayajidda's son born of the Mai's daughter, formed the 'Hausa Bokwa' or seven legitimate Hausa states. It is of further interest that the concubine, Gwari, bore Karbagari, whose seven sons founded and ruled over their own states, namely Kebbi, Yauri, Gwari, Nupe, Kwororofa (Jukun), Zamfara and Yoruba (Ilorin). These latter seven states are known as the Banza Bokwa' meaning the seven bastard or illegitimate Hausa states. This story is told because of its significance to the present Hausa emirate, and because it is possible to visit the well at Daura even today.

The well is in a modern concrete building, but inside it is suitably decorated, with the sword of Bayajidda and a plaque commemorating the killing of the snake. It is said that if you drink from the well, you will always return to Daura. The town is a traditional Hausa 'desert' town and the gate, through which Bayajidda is said to have entered, is still standing. Daura holds a Sallah celebration at all 3 Muslim festivals, *Id-el-Fitri*, *Id-el-Kabir* and *Id-el-Maulud*, although the Durbar is smaller than the one at Katsina. Daura is due north of Kano and due east of Katsina. There is no suitable hotel there, so it is best to stay in Kano.

Route

From Kano, there is a good tarred road due north to Daura.

Gurara Falls

General

Gurara Falls are on the Gurara River in Niger State, on the road between Suleja and Minna. The falls are very impressive in the wet season, but by the end of the dry season they are greatly reduced. They are approximately 200m wide with a drop of about 30m and in the rains they have a large amount of water cascading over the top, creating rainbows in the spray below. You can climb down a steep path to the water's edge beneath the falls, although there is a good viewing spot and covered picnic place where you can take photographs without having to do the climb! There is a plan to develop Gurara into an established tourist site. It is hoped that the charm of this natural, peaceful site will still be preserved. Gurara Falls is well worth a visit for a picnic lunch or even as a camping site, but it is necessary to bring all your own requirements, as the small bar is not always open. The nearest hotels are at Abuja or Minna.

Route

From Abuja, take the northern dual carriageway to the main Kaduna Road. Turn right and shortly after passing Zuma Rock, turn left at a major turning towards Suleja. From Suleja take the Minna Road for approximately 32 km, then shortly after going past the turning to Bida at Lambatta, (about 4 km) you will see a sign on the right saying 'Nigeria's No. 1 Tourist Attraction'. Go down this road for another 4 km and you will come to the top of the falls.

Kaduna

General

Kaduna used to be the colonial capital of Northern Nigeria. It is on the Kaduna River. It has an airport and a railway station and is an important junction with roads branching off in 5 different directions. It is a major communications centre and industrial base in the north, and a thriving modern town. For the tourist, it is an excellent base from which to explore the surrounding countryside, with its many interesting inselbergs and pleasant spots to visit. Anyone living near, or visiting Kaduna for any length of time should try and obtain the British Advisory Team Travel Notes, which were originally started by the author in Kaduna in 1979, but subsequently up-dated by others. These are very helpful and give much greater local detail than is possible in this guide. Within Kaduna, there is little of tourist interest apart from the museum and the market. In the River Gardens there is an old iron footbridge, built in 1880, which was moved from Zungeru, Lord Lugard's former capital, to its present site in the gardens in 1920, when Kaduna became the new capital of the Northern Region.

There is a small National Museum on Ali Akilu Road

with wood carvings, masks and a few examples of Nok terracotta figures and Benin bronzes. There is a craft area with a craft shop behind the museum where you can watch the craftsmen at work. It is open daily from 9.00 am to 6.00 p.m. There are 2 other places with small displays of traditional clothing, etc.: one at the Ministry of Information, Hospital Road, and another at the Secretariat, Sardauna Hall.

A polo tournament is held in Kaduna in October every year and an annual trade fair between January and February. The golf course, Golf Course Road, is an 18-hole championship course.

One 'must' for Kaduna is a visit to the Jacaranda Restaurant and Pottery, which is about 15 to 20 minutes drive south-east from Kaduna, out on the Kachia road. The restaurant is well-managed, has excellent food and drink and is in beautiful garden surroundings, with waterfalls, Japanese style bridges, crocodile ponds and a golf-driving range. The pottery sells first-class pottery designed along similar lines to the Suleja pottery, using natural glazes. There is also a well-run plant nursery, with the plants labelled. The restaurant is open daily for lunch but is only open in the evenings for special functions. Sunday lunch is always a very popular occasion. You will not regret a visit to the restaurant, which is undoubtedly one of the best in Nigeria. There is a proposal to build chalets at the restaurant sometime in the future.

Route

There are 3 alternative routes from Lagos: the shortest is via Ibadan-Ilorin bypass-Jebba-Mokwa-Tegina, and Birnin Gwari-Kaduna. Note that the road, shown on some maps as a dotted line, north of Mokwa to Tegina (cutting off Kontagora) is now complete and a very good road.

However, the stretch of road from Ibadan to just short of Ilorin has many bends and heavy traffic, although there are plans to make it a dual-carriageway sometime in the future. The Ilorin bypass is some 40 km north of Ogbomoso, where there is a junction signed to the left, marked 'Jebba', and this is a good straight road. The journey can be done in about 9 hours. The alternative routes are either via Benin City, Okene and Koton-Karifi or via Ore, Owo, Ipele and north to Kabba along another new road, thence to Koton-Karifi and north along the A2, but this is longer and it is advisable to break your journey overnight en route.

Hotels

Kaduna has 2 modern hotels, the Durbar and Hamdala, which are good. Both are near the Polo Ground to the north of the town, east of the main dual carriageway. The Durbar is on Independence Way, Tel. (062) 201100-8. The Hamdala, which was refurbished in 1989, is on Waff Road, Tel. (062) 211005.

Outside the Hamdala are traders' stalls which sell tourist items, e.g. wood carvings, beads, Fulani blankets, baskets, etc. These are well worth a visit, but be prepared to bargain hard before you purchase.

Kafanchan/Kagoro

Kafanchan and the smaller village of Kagoro are just below the Jos escarpment on the eastern border of Kaduna State. It is a very scenic spot bordered by steep hills. From Kaduna, it is on the southern route to Jos, via Kachia. From Abuja, take the road east to Keffi, and then turn north towards Kachia. Turn right (east), at Kwoi and continue until you reach Kafanchan.

Tourist sites

a. The Waterfall. The fall is over a 'cliff' about 30 m high with a deep pool at the base, and is naturally more impressive in the wet season. It is necessary to walk down the river, along the bank to reach the sandy beach by the falls where there is a pleasant picnic spot. From Kagoro, take the road towards Kafanchan until you come to a roundabout. Turn right along a tarmac road which later becomes laterite. Continue roughly parallel to the railway line, but when in doubt keep right until you reach the top of the falls. The Kaduna State government has plans to develop this site for tourists.

b. Railway engine graveyard. Kafanchan is a railway junction: one line going from Jos to Kaduna and the other going south. Near the railway station are workshops and sidings, and in the sidings are about 10 old steam locomotives. They are rapidly deteriorating, but nevertheless for railway-buffs or small boys this place is well worth a visit. From Kagoro, take the road to Kafanchan, turn left at the roundabout, go past the station, follow the road over the railway, bear left and then follow the road to the right. The old engines can be seen quite clearly. The author last visited this place in 1989 and there were still some good examples of River Class steam-engines, and Canadian diesel locomotives. However, it is important to get permission from the engineer in charge, before entering the engines.

c. Kagoro Boy Scout Camp. Some years ago, a Boy Scout Jamboree was held at Kagoro, and some of the camp still remains. Although the huts are now derelict, it makes a good base for camping, (which we did in 1980), as there is shade and a clean stream for washing. Unfortunately, when we visited it again in 1989, it was very overgrown. It would still be possible to camp if you were prepared to clear the site a little first, as it is a good starting point for walks up the escarpment, and is close to the Kagoro Forest, an excellent place for bird-watching. If you are coming from Kaduna, drive through Kagoro in the direction of Jemma and Jos, and 200 m after the railway crossing at the end of the town, turn left onto a track beside a cactus hedge. Follow the track, cross a wooden bridge and turn right after 700 m by a large tree. Turn left about 300 m further on opposite some houses on the right. Cross another wooden bridge, and you will reach the old Scout Camp; a few minutes with a machete should provide you with a campsite!

d. The Kagoro Forest, a few kilometres down the road towards Jemma and Jos, is a unique area of rainforest of a type not normally found in northern Nigeria, with species of flora and fauna usually seen much further south. This forest is of special interest to bird-watchers and botanists.

Hotels

Kafanchan has a Catering Resthouse, and there is a small hotel in Kagoro, but I have not personally tried it out; so my advice is to camp there in the dry season or to make it a day trip from Jos, about $\frac{1}{2}$ to 2 hours away.

Kano

General

Kano is the largest city in the north but there is a great contrast between the old Hausa city and the modern, industrial one with its international airport and railway station. It is a communications centre with main roads branching out on all points of the compass, joining the other main centres of population in Northern Nigeria. Historically, it has been a centre of trade, especially towards the north across the Sahara and south to Zaria. The Emir of Kano is one of the senior emirs in the north and his palace is in the old part of Kano, near the museum. Kano has much to offer the tourist and the photographer.

Tourist sites

a. The Gidan Makama Museum. The museum is near the Emir's palace and is excellent, as it shows the history of Kano, and the Hausa and Fulani people and some history of the rest of northern Nigeria. It is well worth a visit, not only for its contents, and for its shops selling arts and crafts, but also for the shape and construction of its very old building which is a national monument of architectural excellence. The museum was being renovated when we visited Kano in late 1989.

b. The Dye Pits. The dye pits are by the side of the road at Kofar Mata in Kano. The large vats filled with indigo dye are sunk into the ground, and the dyed cloth is laid out to dry beside them, and then beaten to obtain a high gloss. The full procedure for dyeing the cloth is best explained by one of the guides in the area. Do not take photographs without permission, which will probably require some 'dash'. The pits themselves are a little disappointing, and the area is far from clean, but do not be put off. Ask for a briefing on the dyeing from someone who speaks English and you will be surprised what you learn. Kano is not the only place which has dye-pits, but it is the best known. An alternative to the Kano dye-pits are those at Katsina.

c. Emir's Palace. The Emir's palace is worth a visit, to see the old walls and the entrance gate. Kano is famous for its old walls around the older part of the city. It is 17.5 km in circumference and has 16 gates. One of the best places to see it is near the Central

Gurara Falls, between Suleja and Minna

Jacaranda Restaurant, Kaduna

Entrance to the Emir's Palace, Kano

The Emir of Katsina at the Sallah Festival, Katsina

Mosque (see below). The Emir holds two Sallah festivals each year.

d. Central Mosque. The mosque is one of the largest in Nigeria, and is a fine looking building. With permission, you may be allowed up one of its minarets in order to have a good view of the city below. You are not allowed into the Mosque, itself, unless you are a Muslim, of course.

e. Kurmi Market. There are at least 6 markets in the city, but the Kurmi Market is in the old city. It is worth a visit for those who are not acquainted with northern city markets. The market is at the Makwarari/Dinki Quarters. It sells calabashes, beads, leatherwork, pottery, etc. It is best to have a guide, if possible.

f. Kano Zoo. The Kano Zoo is south of Kano on the Zaria road. It is west of Gyadi-Gyadi village at Gandom Aldasa. The 25 acre zoo is said to be worth a visit, especially for children.

Route

The quickest route to Kano from Lagos, if you do not go by air, is via Kaduna. There is a new dual-carriageway from Kano to Kaduna. This will therefore not only be faster, but safer. The Zaria to Kaduna road had the reputation of being the most dangerous road in Nigeria, but with the new road fully operational this will no longer be the case. The journey from Lagos to Kano is a good 2-day journey as the complete distance is over 1,000 km.

Hotels

There are 2 large hotels in Kano, but neither is particularly new. The Central Hotel is on Bompai Road, Tel. (064) 600520, 621042. Telex 77151 NG CENTEL. The Daula Hotel is at 150M Murtala Mohammed Way. Tel. (064) 600590. An alternative is the Peking Chinese Restaurant in Bompai Road, which also has a limited number of rooms for overnight visitors. Tel. (064) 625146.

Katsina

General

Katsina is one of the northernmost cities in Nigeria. It is on the edge of the Sahel area, bordering the country of Niger, with which it has had historical trading links for many centuries. Katsina is one of the old walled Hausa cities and is the capital of the recently created Katsina State. The city-walls were built by Queen Amina in the 16th century and have 7 gates. The gate through which Lord Lugard entered Katsina in 1903 is known as Kofar Yandaka, and a plaque commemorates the occasion. The Goborau Minaret is probably the most picturesque tourist attraction. It is the tallest mud-brick building in Nigeria and is said to be about 250 years old. A fine view of Katsina can be gained from the top, but please get permission to enter the minaret beforehand. The Emir of Katsina holds a most colourful and interesting Sallah during Muslim festivals of *Id-el-Fitri* (end of Ramadan) and *Id-el-Kabir*. The respective dates of these two festivals depend upon the sighting of a new moon and are declared by the Sultan of Sokoto. The dates vary each year, but an English Letts diary can help your planning, as it marks the quarters of the moon. In the case of *Id-el-Fitri*, it is normally 30 days from the beginning of Ramadan. In 1992, the Sallah was in early April which gives a rough guide.

The Sallah at Katsina includes a procession of horsemen and camels, acrobats, jugglers, snake charmers and various other entertainers. At Katsina a spectacular charge (or 'jahi') by the chiefs and courtiers on horseback is included, as a salute to the Emir. The celebrations normally start at about 8.00 am. with the brilliantly attired horsemen arriving in the main square in front of the Emir's Palace. They then gather outside the city walls for prayers before returning at about 10.00 am. The Emir and his retinue enter the square and when all are assembled, the charge takes place, after which the Emir gives a short oration and then retires to his palace. The festival continues in the square with dancing, music and other traditional activities.

Route

The best route from Lagos is via Kaduna-Zaria-Funtua-Mulumfashi-Yash-Katsina. It is possible to make the journey in 2 days, but it is hard driving. From Kaduna it is about 5½ – 6 hours. An alternative is to fly to the new airport opened in 1991.

Hotels

The Liyafa Palace Hotel was opened in 1991 and is of high standard. The only alternative is the Katsina Guest Inn which is adequate. It is possible to drive from Kano, but it means a very early start.

Koton-Karifi

Koton-Karifi is known for its bridge across the River Niger. It is a fine example of engineering owing to its length and width. Koton-Karifi is just north of Lokoja (where the Niger and Benue rivers meet) on the main road to Abuja from Benin City.

Kazaure

Kazaure is one of the northern emirates. It is a pleasant Hausa town with an Emir's palace, but on a smaller scale than most, and is about 1 hour's drive due north of Kano.

A good view of the town can be had from the hill behind the town. The market is held on a Friday. It is only worth visiting if you are passing that way, but for bird-watchers there are some interesting wetlands nearby.

Minna

General

Minna is the capital of Niger State and is on the main railway line from Lagos to Kaduna and the north, and has a small airport. It does not have many tourist sites itself except a new cultural centre, a small pottery and a museum, but there are several places of interest nearby. At the railway station, there is an old railway engine on display, which has been kept in good condition to commemorate the fact that Minna was an important railway junction in the past. A potential tourist site is the large hydro-electric dam and power station at Shiroro Dam, on the Kaduna River, north-east of Minna. Take the Owada Road and continue due north over the railway line to the dam, but it is necessary to get permission from NEPA first. *See* page 89 for directions of Gurara Falls, an hour or more from Minna in the direction of Abuja.

Minna has recently had an extensive road-building programme and there is now a direct road to Bida. In the future, it is hoped to have a good direct road to Kaduna, up the line of the Kaduna River. There has been a bypass constructed round the south of Minna.

Route

From Lagos the route is Ibadan-Ilorin (or Ilorin bypass)-Jebba-Mokwa-Bida-Minna. The road from Bida to Minna shown as a dotted line on some maps is now complete. From Bida, the turn-off to Minna is clearly marked to the left, a few kilometres outside the town, on the Lapai Road. Do not take the old road via Wushishi unless you have plenty of time to spare!

Hotels

The Shiroro Hotel on the newly-constructed bypass is the best hotel in Minna. Tel. (016) 222021 or 222498

Sokoto

General

Sokoto is the centre of Islamic activities in Nigeria. It is the home of the Sultan of Sokoto, the spiritual leader of Muslims in the country. It is also the capital of Sokoto State. The city is well-laid out with avenues of neem trees, wide roads and large roundabouts, and seems like an oasis in a semi-desert area. The area around the river is an attractive place to walk in the evening, with fishermen bringing in their nets and herdsmen watering their herds. Sokoto is another of the great trading cities of the north, with old trade routes across the Sahara to Morocco and Algeria. It is famed for its excellent leatherwork including handbags, pouffes, wallets, fans, etc. Sokoto has an airport and it is also one of the main starting points for the drive across the Sahara to North Africa and Europe.

The old Sokoto market was burnt down, but there is now a modern central market. It is still very colourful and has many items of interest, e.g. Fulani blankets, leatherwork, beads, rush mats and other handicrafts, many coming from Niger across the border. There is also a camel market, and camels are a frequent sight in Sokoto State. The old part of the town is full of character and you may see snake charmers at work.

Tourist sites

a. The Sultan's Palace. The palace is worth a visit to see

the building and the guards in their multicoloured robes. At 9.00 pm on Thursdays, you can watch the musicians and praise-singers honour the Sultan. The palace is on Sultan Bello Road, to the north-east of the old town of Sokoto. The present Sultan, His Excellency, Alhaji Ibrahim Dasuki is a descendant of Usman dan Fodio, the first Sultan.

b. Usman dan Fodio's Tomb. Usman dan Fodio led the Fulani Jihad against King Yunfa, the Hausa ruler of Gobir, in 1804. The Fulani came from Senegal and were in the minority to the Hausa at the time of the uprising. Both the town and nomadic cattle Fulani joined together because they feared that they might be driven out by the Hausa. Usman dan Fodio was concerned that the Hausa were not strict Muslims and wished to see that some of their pagan ways were eliminated. The jihad was successful because the Hausa rulers were not united and by 1808 all the main rulers in Zaria, Daura, Kano, Bauchi, Gobir, Katsina, Kebbi and Zamfara had been defeated. The jihad spread to Adamawa, Nupe and Ilorin, but failed to succeed in Borno. Usman dan Fodio's tomb is, therefore, of great significance to Muslims in Nigeria. It is not a tourist site as such, but of great historical importance. Women are not allowed inside the tomb, and you should ask for permission if you wish to photograph the entrance. For more information, read *Essentials of West African History, Book One*, by J Akin Akinyemi.

c. Sokoto Museum. The present Sokoto Museum is in the History Bureau not far from the Sultan's palace. It is worth a visit if you are interested in the history of Northwest Nigeria.

d. Clapperton's Tomb. Clapperton, the great English explorer, who was accompanied by Richard Lander, died in Sokoto and was buried there. This will be of interest to historians. Anyone interested should ask for further information at the History Bureau.

Route

The shortest route to Sokoto by road is Lagos-Ibadan-Ilorin-(or Ilorin bypass)-Jebba-Kontagora-Yelwa- Jega-Sokoto. This is a 2-day journey. The alternative route, if you are travelling via Abuja, is Kaduna-Zaria-Funtua-Gusau-Sokoto, but of course this is much longer. An alternative is to fly.

Hotels

Sokoto has a number of hotels. The most modern is the Giginya which was completed in 1988. It is on the Bye-Pass Road, not far from the airport. Tel. (060) 231263, 231670. The other good hotel is the Shakura Hotel which is closer to the centre of the town, and the older Sokoto Hotel is next door.

Suleja

General

Suleja is famous for the Ladi Kwali Pottery, which used to be known as the Abuja Pottery before the town was renamed 'Suleja'. The pottery was set up with the help of Michael Cardew, and Dr Ladi Kwali, was his renowned pupil. The pottery staff are happy to show visitors around and you can purchase pottery either in its finished glazed state or in the 'terracotta' stage. The pottery is of a high standard and the traditional designs are most interesting. One of the women potters we met had the designs of lizards, snakes, and butterflies tattooed on her arms. It is worth a visit and should not be missed if you are visiting either Abuja or Minna.

Route

Suleja is on the Abuja-Minna Road just to the west of the main road (A2) which runs from Lokoja to Kaduna. Enter Suleja along the main road from the A2, turn left (south) into the main street at the T-junction, and continue along this road, over a narrow bridge and you will see the pottery on your left shortly afterwards. It has a sign outside it, but if you are in doubt, ask, it is well-known.

Wurno

Wurno is 30 km north-east of Sokoto on the Rima River. It is a large Hausa village made exclusively of mud bricks on a rocky outcrop overlooking the river. Its claim to fame is the tomb of Sultan Bello.

Zaria

General

Zaria is one of the original walled Hausa cities, founded in the 16th century. It is an attractive city which has retained its ancient looks to some degree by leaving most of the modern development and industry to Kaduna nearby! It was once surrounded by approximately 19 km of walls which in some areas are still well-preserved. The Zaria area used to be part of the ancient kingdom of Zazzia, but it was renamed Zaria in honour of the Chief's wife. Zaria has 2 important establishments: the Ahmadu Bello University at Samaru on the Sokoto Road, founded in 1962, which was the first university in the north of the country, and the Regimental Depot of the Nigerian Army on Kaduna Road. The depot has the Regimental Museum of the Nigerian Army. Zaria has a splendid Sallah, especially at *Id-el-Fitri*. The old town has many very decorative buildings, including the Emir's palace and the central mosque (a replica of which can be seen in the

Zuma Rock near Abuja

Flower of the Baobab tree *(Adansonia digitata)*

Rocks near Gwoza

Riyom Rocks near Jos

Museum of Architecture at Jos). Some traditional crafts are still carried on in Zaria, and it is possible to see the blacksmiths and the potters at work.

Route

Zaria old town is to the right of the main Kaduna-Kano Road. (For directions from Lagos to Kaduna, *see* page 90.) If you go into the town you will not be disappointed.

Hotels

Zaria is only an hour's journey north of Kaduna, so it is probably best to use the hotels in Kaduna (*see* page 91), but there is also The Conference Hotel, at Kongo, near the university.

Zuma Rock

The Zuma Rock is one of the natural landmarks of Nigeria. It is an enormous inselberg or granite rock, standing out from the surrounding countryside like a giant stone altar. It even has the semblance of a face etched on it when you approach it from the south. The rock itself is about 1km long and several hundred metres high, with sheer rock faces on all sides carved into vertical lines by centuries of heavy rainfall running down from the summit in the wet season. It makes a spectacular photograph. A hotel is being constructed at the foot of the rock, which hopefully will not intrude upon the view. The rock can be seen on the right soon after you pass the northern turn-off to Abuja (the dual carriageway) on the A2 Road between Lokoja and Kaduna. It cannot be mistaken for any other inselberg.

Zungeru

General

Zungeru was Lord Lugard's northern capital. There are still a few signs of his occupation left, including the old bridge across a tributary of the Kaduna River, the old garrison church, some war-graves and the ruins of some buildings. The Niger State government has plans to renovate some of the historical areas so visitors can see them more readily. When this work is completed, it will be of special interest to historians. If you are passing that way there is a scenic bridge across the Kaduna River which passes through a gorge with curious rock formations. The old bridge is shared by motor vehicles and the railway, which is somewhat unusual, but a new road-bridge was opened at the end of 1989 a few kilometres further north on the Tegina-Minna Road. The direct route no longer goes through Zungeru. There are plans to dam the Kaduna River nearby. If these plans are carried out, Zungeru may change from a quiet town, to that of a bustling industrial area.

Route

Zungeru is on the old Minna—Tegina Road in Niger State. There are no hotels in the town, but *see* page 99 on Minna. To reach the historical sites, coming from Minna on the old road, turn right in the centre of the town off the main road, and it is another 1-2 km further on, across the small bridge on a tributary of the Kaduna River. We found an elderly man who acted as our guide and was very helpful as he was old enough to remember something of the town's history.

Zurgurma Sector of the Lake Kainji National Park

The Zurgurma Sector of the National Park is to be

developed by the Niger State government. This should include offices, chalets and game-viewing tracks. *See* Lake Kainji National Park, page 35.

5
North-east

Introduction

General

North-east Nigeria is the area north of the Benue River, bordered in the north and east by the countries of Niger, Cameroon and Chad, and in the west by the state boundaries of Kano and Kaduna. It includes the states of Plateau, Bauchi, Jigawa, Yobe, Borno and the northern part of Adamawa State. It, therefore, has such sharply contrasting landscapes as the picturesque Jos Plateau which rises to over 1,219 m, the Mandara Mountains running down the border with Cameroon, and the flat, low-lying, Lake Chad basin.

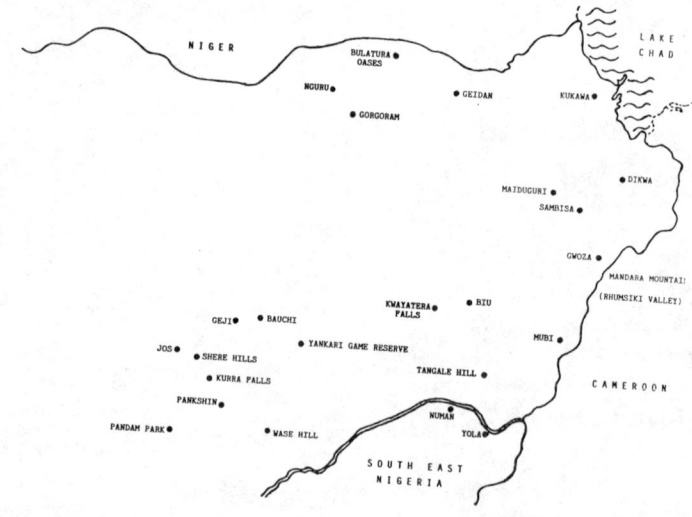

Many centuries ago, when Lake Chad was a great deal larger, much of the north-east corner of Borno was under the waters of the lake. The north-east also includes the wetlands of Hadejia-Nguru. In the far north of Yobe State there are the ever-encroaching sands of the Sahara desert. One can see rolling dunes and oases. The people are of many ethnic groups and religions, although they are predominantly Muslim, but this region is sparsely populated in comparison with the south. Because of the distance, it is not often visited by people from Lagos, except for well-known places like Jos and the Yankari Game Reserve. For this reason, many of the tourist sites are undeveloped, but the area should not be neglected by the keen traveller, as it has much to offer, and has some of the most scenic areas in Nigeria.

Bauchi

General

Bauchi town is the fast-growing capital of Bauchi State. It is surrounded by some attractive hills, and can be used as a base to visit both the Yankari Game Reserve, which is about 1½ hours away to the south-east, and the Geji Rock Paintings (*See* page 110) which are on the Bauchi-Jos Road. Bauchi only has a small airport, suitable for private planes, so the nearest main airport is at Jos. Bauchi is on the main Jos-Maiduguri railway line and is served by roads from Kano, Jos, Maiduguri and Yola.

Tourist sites

a. Bauchi State Museum. The state museum is in Bauchi exactly opposite the Zaranda Hotel on the Jos Road. It has pottery, stone age tools, weapons and masks. It is a small but interesting museum which was opened in 1988. It is open every day except Sundays from 7.00 am to 5.30 pm.

b. Tafawa Balewa's Tomb. The tomb of the first Prime Minister of Nigeria, Abubakar Tafawa Balewa, is a simple but impressive monument. Behind it is a historical section with a library showing videos of Independence Day and some of the personal effects of the late Prime Minister, who left this earth with very little he could call his own apart from his small family farm. The memorial to this great man epitomises his simple, dedicated and loyal life as a teacher, prime minister and leader of Nigeria until he was killed in Nigeria's first coup. The tomb is at Ran Road, (Old Maiduguri Road), Bauchi. It is open from 8.00 am to 6.00 pm from Monday to Friday and from 8.00 am to 12.00 noon on Saturdays.

Route

The best route to Bauchi is Lagos-Ajaokuta (the new bridge across the Niger)-Makurdi-Jos-Bauchi.

Hotels

The Zaranda Hotel can be clearly seen on the right, coming from Jos, shortly before entering the town. It is a tall cream-coloured building close to the road. It is a modern hotel with a swimming pool, seldom in working order and has an excellent view of the surrounding countryside. There is a Yankari booking office in the reception hall. Tel. (077) 42480. There is also the Awalah Hotel on the junction of the roads to Kano and Kari a few kilometres north of Bauchi, which is less expensive than the Zaranda.

Bulatura Oases

The Bulatura Oases are in Yobe State, north-east of Nguru. The area is the 'desert' of the Hollywood film—set dunes, camels, and palm trees around an oasis. To visit this area, it is necessary to have a 4-wheel drive vehicle which is prepared for operating in such conditions, and essential to have a guide, but the area is most attractive, and an experience for those who have not been in the desert before. The oases are also excellent for bird-watchers and in the dry season there are thousands of Palaearctic migrants wintering there. The Project Officer at the headquarters of the Hadejia-Nguru Wetlands Project in Nguru, could advise you (*See* page 120 on Nguru). There is no modern hotel at Nguru, but very basic accommodation is available at either the Nguru Guest Inn or the Green Garden Hotel. Although the accommodation is better at the former, the food is reputed to be better at the latter. It is also possible to camp either at the Project Headquarters, with the permission of the Project Officer, or at the Oases themselves. From Nguru, the first part of the route is along the Maiduguri Road, until you reach the village of Jajimaji. From here, the road is a sandy track all the way to the Oases which is over an hour's journey. As stated earlier, a guide is necessary as there are many tracks. It would be easy to lose one's way. This trip is only recommended for the traveller who is used to rugged conditions.

Dikwa

Dikwa, in Borno State, was where the Shehu (King) of Dikwa, a marauder from the Sudan, lived at the beginning of this century. There is an interesting mudbrick fort in the town which is being restored by the National Museum. The Shehu's tomb is nearby, but has not yet been restored. The fort is chiefly of interest to historians, and there is a small but colourful market in the village where you can see Kanuri women with their decorative hairstyles. The old German DC's house is still standing. Dikwa is about one hour's drive due east of Maiduguri along the A3 which is a good road. The surrounding landscape is a flat, barren, thorn-bush country, and camel-trains are not an unusual sight.

Geidam

Geidam is in the very north of Yobe State, north-west of Maiduguri, and is an old desert city which has seen better days. Nearby is the old city of Birnin N'Gazargamo which was the capital of Borno at the beginning of the 19th century. It was sacked by the Fulani jihadists and is now only a ruin of scattered bricks. The route to Geidam from Maiduguri is north via Gubio. A few kilometres before Damasak the road becomes a sandy track and from there to Geidam it is only possible in a 4-wheel drive vehicle, with a guide, as it is a poorly defined desert track. It is recommended for the adventurous traveller.

Geji Rock Paintings

The Geji Rock Paintings are at Dutseen Sare near Geji in Bauchi State, on the Bauchi—Jos Road. The paintings are like those at Birnin Kudu (*see* page 85), not all that clear nor particularly large or impressive. However, they are of interest to historians, because they are considered to be about 800 years old. There is a red sign on the left of the main road about 24 km from Bauchi. If coming from Jos, the red sign is on the right close to the 474 km stone to Maiduguri. A track leads to the right (coming from Bauchi) off the main road northwards for 6½ km to the settlement of Dutseen Sare. From here the local boys will guide you, for a suitable sum, the ½ km from the primary school to the Geji inselberg, where you will see a caged area protecting the paintings. The latter part of the track is

Kamale Pinnacle, Mandara Mountains

Camel in semi-desert sahel zone, Nguru

Lioness in Yankari Game Reserve

Wikki Warm Springs, Yankari Game Reserve

only suitable for four-wheel drive vehicles.

This area is also notable for its women who extend their lips by placing coins or round objects in them, but never photograph the women without first asking their permission. The best base for a visit to Geji is either Jos or Bauchi, but Bauchi is the nearest.

Gorgoram

Gorgoram is the old walled town which was once the capital of the Bade Emirate. It lies in the middle of the Hadejia wetlands surrounded by 'fadama' which host thousands of birds. A good contact is the primary school teacher who may find you a guide, or ask for the Forestry/Wildlife staff. If you are based in Nguru, the NCF representative at the Hadejia-Nguru Wetlands Project could advise you on the state of the roads, etc. The only way to get there is through Gashua, on the route between Nguru and Maiduguri. From Gashua take a minor road in a south-west direction.

Gwoza Hills

Gwoza is south-east of Maiduguri on the main road to Yola. The hills to the south and east of Gwoza along the Cameroon border are very scenic, and there is a fortified town south of Madagali called Sukor, about 25 km south of Gwoza. Ask in the area for directions. Sukor is very interesting, as, in addition to the fortifications, it is one of the few places where the people smelt their own iron to make tools, as filmed by the Basil Davidson 'Africa' team. It is about 1½ hours walk up a remarkable stone-built 'pathway'. From Gwoza, there is a shorter walk/climb into the hills from the valley behind the town, which goes to the village of Guduf, where there are interesting 'bone' huts. Park by the primary school in the valley.

Jos

General

Jos has always been a popular place with Europeans because of its height above sea level, (1,219 m), cool evenings, unique rocky scenery of the plateau and the many tourist sites to visit. It is the capital of Plateau State and is served by roads going north, south, east and west, by the railway and an airport. It has 2 golf courses, Rayfield and Plateau, a Polo club and numerous other forms of sport and entertainment. Jos used to be an important tin mining centre, and mining can be observed at Bukuru to the south of the city.

Tourist sites

a. National Museum, Museum of Architecture and Zoo. The National Museum in Jos is one of the best in Nigeria, especially for archaeology and pottery. It has many fine examples of Nok terracotta heads and artefacts, which were discovered in Plateau State and date from between 500 BC and 200 AD. The Pottery Hall has an exceptionally good collection of pots from all over the country. The museum of architecture is in the same grounds and is on the right as you drive into the museum car park. It contains life-size replicas of the different forms of Nigerian architecture, from the walls of Kano to the Mosque at Zaria and a Tiv village. The Zoo is next to the National Museum and is of interest to children. It is one of the best in the country. The museum is in the residential area, off Legal Drive quite close to the Hill Station Hotel. Ask for directions from the hotel staff.

b. Jos Wildlife Park. The wildlife park does not compare with similar parks in Europe or America, but it is attractively set out and of interest to those who enjoy seeing animals, and of course, to children. It is 8 sq.

Kurra Falls

General

The Kurra Falls themselves can only be seen in the wet season when there is plenty of water, as they do not exist in the dry season. However, the surrounding area is very scenic in the dry season and is a pleasant picnic or camping spot. The author camped there in 1980, and greatly enjoyed the splendid views of typical 'Scottish' scenery with hills, lakes and moors. The area is the property of NESCO, an electrical company whose head office is in Bukuru, near Jos. The Kurra Falls area is very attractive, has fine walks and a variety of birdlife. If you have time during a visit to Jos, do not miss this day's outing.

Route

From Jos take the main road south and at the roundabout take the Pankshin Road to Barakin Ladi (24 km from the roundabout). Fork right off the main road at a sign reading 'Kurra Falls'. Pass the General Hospital on your left, drive on for 3 km and turn right at another sign to the falls. Drive another 27 km along a good road to Kurra Falls village. Report to the NESCO office on the right, or if that is closed, to the police for permission to enter the area. Ask for a guide if you want to see the falls, otherwise proceed through the village taking a left fork until you meet a barrier where you turn right and cross a bridge on the outskirts of the village. Drive on up the road to another barrier, which is manned by a NESCO employee. The road continues for a further 10 km from the village, past the reservoirs. You can stop and choose your ideal picnic spot somewhere along this road.

Kwayatera Waterfall

The Kwayatera Waterfall is about 30 km from Biu on the Gombe to Biu Road, east of Bauchi. It is best visited during the wet season, say July to September, when there will be plenty of water running. As you drive south from Biu, look for the signboard pointing to the irrigation scheme and also for the track to the right. Take this track and turn left to the waterfall before you reach the irrigation scheme, about 2 km from the road. Park at the top of the fall, and the path to the bottom is downstream. A four-wheel drive vehicle is recommended in the wet season.

Lake Chad Area

Lake Chad would appear on the map as a huge expanse of water—one imagines plenty of fishing boats and bird and animal life in abundance. But due to the recent droughts, Lake Chad has shrunk considerably and the Nigerian part of the lake consists mostly of marshes. However, as a result of heavy rains there was again some water in the lake in 1989 and the bird-life returned in large numbers. It would be wise to take up-to-date advice from the headquarters of the Lake Chad Development Authority in Maiduguri or from Baba Grema, Chief Wildlife Officer in the Forestry Department in the State Secretariat, before attempting to visit the area. They can advise you of the route via Baga which is some kilometres from the lake along a canal, but the distance varies enormously with the level of water in the lake. From Maiduguri, the first part of the route is via Dikwa and Monguno. For the best route to Maiduguri *see* page 120.

Mandara Mountains (See Rhumsiki Valley on page 123).

km of unspoilt savannah bush, and the rare pigmy hippopotamus is successfully being bred here in a 'hippo pool'. The lions are in a large enclosure simulating their natural habitat, and there are elephants, a red river hog, jackal, a chimpanzee, monkeys, crocodiles and other animals. There is a watch-tower at the top of Vong Nfwei Hill, the highest point in the park (1,345 m) with an excellent view of Jos and the surrounding area, where it would be possible to picnic, but the road up to it is not in very good condition. However, apart from the park, there are caged animals near the offices, which you can visit on foot. The park opens at 10.00 am. and the charges are minimal. The route to the Park from the Hill Station Hotel is as follows: take the dual carriageway towards Bukuru and after passing the very obvious red and white Nasco factory on your left, you will see Miango Road on your right, signed to the Park. After travelling 4 km, you will see the entrance to the Park on your right.

c. The Shere Hills. The Shere Hills are the hills that can be seen to the east of Jos. One way of getting to the hills is to turn right off the eastern bypass to Bauchi, where it curves to the left, bear right (east) up towards the Plateau Golf Club, and continue on into the hills. It is a scenic area for walks and picnics. Go prepared with plenty of water, haversack rations and good walking shoes. As always when walking in the 'bush', take careful note of your route! For more details of the area, seek local advice.

d. Jos Ultra-Modern Market. The Jos market is a purpose-built modern market with 4,290 stalls, car park and other services such as banks and a post office. The market is worth a visit. It is on the Bauchi road, in the centre of the town just below the residential area.

e. Naraguta Leatherworks and Pottery. The leatherworks are at Naraguta village, past the Jos University hostel on the Bauchi Road, where articles such as handbags, shoes, pouffes and briefcases can be bought. Decorative pots are on sale in the main street of the village. Take the turning to the left just after the AUN Petrol Station. A sign to the Union of Road Transport Workers marks the turning which is a few kilometres from Jos.

Jos, as a centre for tourism, has much to offer in the surrounding area, all within a day's drive there and back.

Other Tourist sites

a. Assop Falls. This is a small waterfall, (best seen in the wet season) which could make a pleasant picnic spot on a drive from Jos to Abuja, about 64 km from Jos. It is a few kilometres before Gimi, (the turn-off to Akwanga and Abuja), and is signed on the right of the road after descending a steep hill from the plateau. There is a parking area, off the road, and a small charge for entry.

b. Riyom Rock. This pile of rocks is a photographer's dream. It is a dramatic pile of rocks balanced on top of one another, with one looking like a clown's hat, perched precariously on the top. The rocks can be seen on the main Jos-Gimi Road on the right, coming from Jos. After passing by Bukuru and Vom, the road drops between embankments to cross a bridge. Soon afterwards you will see this strange pile of rocks on your right near a village with cactus hedges—a typical feature of this area.

c. Kurra Falls. This is a very pleasant area for walks and picnics, with scenery similar to the Scottish highlands. It is south-west of Jos on the road towards Panyam. *See* page 117.

d. Wase Rock or Hill. This is an impressive inselberg with sheer sides which rises 250 m above the surrounding countryside which is close to Langtang and 216 km from Jos (*see* page 125).

e. Pandam Wildlife Park. This is a rather undeveloped game reserve between Shendam and Lafia on the right of the road. It is approximately 300 km from Jos (see page 122).

f. The Mado Tourist Village is close to the Jos Wildlife Park. This is not fully completed but consists of accommodation and a restaurant.

There are a number of projects planned for tourists around Jos, but as at 1991 they had not been completed. They are the Health Resort at Kerang springs, and the Rock Hotel at Liberty Dam.

Route

The best route from Lagos is via Abuja then to Akwanga, Gimi and Jos, but it is a 2-day journey. The best advice is to have an overnight stop at the Abuja Hilton which is a day's drive, leaving only a morning's journey for the second day. From Kaduna there are 2 routes, the northern, A11, or the southern route, A235, via Kachia and Kagoro. The northern route is the shortest but the southern route is the more scenic. The northern route was badly potholed in 1991.

Hotels

Jos has 2 large hotels, the Hill Station Hotel, 10 Tudun Wada Road, Tel.: (073) 55300–2, 52808, 54817, and the Plateau Hotel, 2 Rest House Road, Tel.: (073) 55740. Both are in the centre of the residential area of Jos, on high ground over-looking the town. The Hill Station Hotel had a new annexe opened in 1988, and is the recommended of the two but the Mountain's Green Hotel is a good alternative. It is on Tudun Wada Ring Road, P.O. Box 1556, Tel.(073) 57033 or 57373. For those who wish to eat out, the Andulusia Restaurant, which is Lebanese owned, has been recommended. It is on the right of the dual carriageway going towards Bukuru.

Kukawa

General

Kukawa is a town close to Lake Chad in Borno State. Its only claim to fame is the tomb of El-Kanemi, the warrior who, on two occasions, assisted the Mai (King) of Borno to quell the Fulani uprisings and then undertook military campaigns around the kingdom of Borno to stop the Fulani from winning back Borno's former vassals and make safe the borders of the kingdom. El-Kanemi was also a Muslim scholar who adhered strictly to the faith, a skilful diplomat and a clever politician. He was the founder of the Shehu (Kanemi) dynasty in Borno and built his new capital at Kukawa in 1814. He died in 1835. There is not a great deal left of the tomb to see, but it is an interesting and historical area to visit.

Route

From Maiduguri the direct road to Monguna has been rehabilitated so you do not have to go via Dikwa. From Monguna take the road north to Kauwa then turn left to Kukawa. If you wish to do the round trip back to Maiduguri, there is a good road to Damasak, but there is no accommodation there. For the first few kilometres from Damasak to Gubio the road becomes a sandy track, but most of the way to Maiduguri, it is good tarmac. It would be wise to take up-to-date advice about the state of these roads before leaving Maiduguri.

conditioners and the generator only goes on at 6.00 pm when it is working. However, if one were prepared with a camping stove and food, it would be possible to semi-camp there at present, but the State Government intends developing it further. It is within reach of a long day-trip from either Jos (via Akwanga) or Abuja. The Lafia Hotel, on the right of the Shendam Road just outside Lafia town, could be a possible overnight stop.

Pankshin

Pankshin is 120 km south-east of Jos on the Jos Plateau, 30 km from Panyam. The Pankshin Hotel is set on a hill with fine views of the surrounding countryside but in 1991 was in need of refurbishment. The gardens must have been superb in the past. There is a pleasant walk around the hill behind the hotel. The town is known for its pottery, especially for its pots which taper at the bottom. It is a very attractive area with many panoramic views, excellent walks and scenic drives.

Rhumsiki Valley

The Rhumsiki Valley is an area of impressive inselbergs in the Mandara Mountain range, north-east of Mubi in the very north of Adamawa State, along the Cameroon border. The area has fantastic volcanic plugs standing up like giant pillars from the surrounding rugged countryside. One of the well-known peaks in the area is the Kamale Pinnacle, featured in Peter Holmes's book, *Nigeria, Giant of Africa*. It is like an enormous finger pointing towards the sky. Either Yola or Maiduguri might be used as a base. To obtain a good view of the Kamale pinnacle, go to the village of Michika on the way from Yola, mid-way between Yola and Maiduguri, turn right (east) at the sign saying 'Government Junior Secondary School, Garta', and continue on the laterite track for several kilometres until you can get a good view of the pinnacle. The first part of the track is suitable for ordinary cars, but further on, a 4-wheel drive vehicle is essential. Remember that this area is very close to the border, and you may be required to prove your identity.

Shere Hills

See Jos page 113

Sambisa Game Reserve

The Sambisa Game Reserve is included in this guide for those who are interested in the flora and fauna of the far north-east of the country. The reserve is south-east of Maiduguri towards Bama, to the right of the road. It is not marked, and, therefore, it is absolutely necessary to have a guide. If you wish to visit this area, contact the Chief Wildlife Officer in the Forestry Department in the State Secretariat in Maiduguri or one of his assistants. They will be willing to help you. The reserve has big game including elephants and many birds like ostriches, marabou storks, tawny eagles and the magnificent bateleur. We were lucky enough to see a secretary bird. The reserve has no accommodation or facilities, but is within easy reach of Maiduguri.

Tangale Hill

Tangale Hill in Bauchi State can be seen quite clearly from the road when you drive from Gombe towards Numan. The hill is a volcanic plug and can be climbed with a guide after getting permission from the Emir of Kaltungo. The climb is over 5 hours. The area is good for walking. The best base is either Bauchi or Yola. No doubt, some accommodation could be found in Gombe or Numan, e.g.

a company guest house, but there are no modern hotels in either place. There is a Catering Rest House in Gombe, but we have not visited it.

Wase Hill

Wase Hill or Rock, as it is sometimes called, in Plateau State, is a remarkable rock rising 250 m perpendicularly out of the surrounding area. It is chiefly of interest to geologists and mountain climbers, but the rock has many legends surrounding it. One of them is that an emir was said to have offered a reprieve to 2 murderers if they climbed to the top. One fell on the way up and was killed, the other reached the top but died of exhaustion. The rock was climbed in 1959 by a Mr P T Wallace, who planted the flag of the Emir of Wase on the summit. Another expedition led by a Mr Wilkinson ended in disaster when a swarm of bees attacked the climbing team, and he was unfortunately stung to death. A game reserve has recently been declared around the rock to protect its fauna. There are white pelicans' nests on the top of the rock, and this is the only known breeding site in Nigeria. Climbing the rock is only allowed in August and September, in order to protect these graceful birds. The route from Jos is south-east to Panyam, east to Pankshin (see page 123) and Amper, south to Langtang, then finally south-east to Wase, which is approximately 220 km from Jos and 100 km from Pankshin. The rock can be seen clearly from Langtang and is only about 25 minutes from there along a good road. A suitable hotel for an overnight stop in Langtang is the Tim Tali Motel on Wase Road. P.O. Box 57. Tel. (070) 52425.

Yankari Game Reserve

General

Yankari Game Reserve and the Wikki Warm Springs are approximately 1½ hours drive south-east of Bauchi. The reserve is the best in Nigeria, but does not compare with the facilities at game reserves in East Africa. There is much work to be done on accommodation, water supply, electricity, the restaurant and other essential facilities to bring it up to international tourist standards. However, in spite of this, it is well worth a visit, particularly if you know what to expect and are not looking for luxury!

The game reserve was set up in 1956 and was opened to the public in 1962. It is based around the Gagi River which is the main game-viewing area. It is open all the year although in the wet season some of the tracks are impassable. The best time of the year to visit is from November to May, but the closer you are to the end of the dry season the more game you are likely to see, as the vegetation has died down and the animals concentrate around the river. Even so, game-viewing trips can be very variable—one morning we saw practically nothing, yet in the evening of the same day large numbers of birds and animals were on show. Once, we saw 16 different species of animal on one game run. Game runs are generally better in the evening as the game come down to the river to drink after the heat of the day.

The Warm Springs at Wikki Camp are one of the best features of the game reserve. They are flood-lit at night, and it is wonderful, after a hot day's game-viewing to relax in the warm water. The spring gushes out from under a cliff, where the water is at least 2 m deep, and the bathing area extends for about 200m to a large sandy beach. Beware of the baboons, who may steal your clothing and valuables unless you keep a look-out. They have also been known to get into chalets and cars to steal food, and can be dangerous, so take care of young children, especially. They are extremely cunning animals.

   The animals that are most often seen in the reserve are elephant, baboon, waterbuck, bushbuck, duiker, oribi, crocodile, hippopotamus, roan antelope, buffalo and warthog (although both the latter species are less common since an epidemic of rinderpest killed many of them), and various types of monkeys. Lions are occasionally seen, but they are so well-camouflaged that in nine visits we have only seen them once. The birds are many and varied, including the huge saddlebill stork, goliath heron, bateleur eagle, fish eagle, vultures, kingfishers, bee-eaters, etc., so it is excellent for keen bird-watchers. You can either go game-viewing in the Yankari transport, or take your own car with a guide, but a 4-wheel drive is advisable, as some of the roads are badly maintained. The tsetse fly can be a nuisance, so take some insect repellent. Always take plenty of water on these trips, because if the car breaks down, you must wait in the vehicle until the guide obtains help, which could take some time.

   It is not particularly cheap to visit Yankari as there are entrance fees to pay at the entrance to the park, (about 43 km from Wikki Camp), and charges for the use of cameras, especially video cameras, and with a family the charges can mount up. The entrance fees are higher for weekends and public holidays. There is no charge for the use of the warm springs, unless you are a day visitor, but this is minimal. It is better to book game runs in advance when you arrive, to ensure that there will be a guide available.

   There are tennis courts and a squash court for the sports enthusiast, and a small museum in the reception area. There is a Mobil petrol pump at Wikki Camp, but it seldom has petrol, fill up with petrol in Bauchi although it is advisable to carry extra cans as there is often a petrol shortage in Bauchi.

Bookings. It is advisable to book for holidays and weekends, and Easter is a particularly popular time. You can either book at the Zaranda Hotel in Bauchi or send a courier letter to Yankari Game Reserve. The most reliable method, as always, is to ask a friend who is going there before you, to make your booking—but how often does this happen when you need it?

Route

The best route from Lagos is via Abuja where you can make an overnight stop, and then to Jos and Bauchi, as it is a 2-day journey by car. From Bauchi take the Gombe road (towards Yola). After approximately 40 km, you cross a bridge over the Gongola River. Turn right at the sign to Yankari Game Reserve almost immediately after crossing the bridge, through the village of Dindima. Wikki Camp is 72 km from the main road, although the entrance to the park is reached after about 30km. The road to the camp was broken up in 1991 and unless it has been repaired, is badly potholed. The roads within the park when you go on game-viewing runs are entirely laterite and are rough in places.

Hotels

The accommodation is in chalets or rondavels and is rather basic. It is advisable to inspect your rooms before accepting them. There is no electricity during the day, thus no water until 6.00 pm when the generator is turned on. However, if you keep the buckets in the bathroom, filling this is no great problem. The Wikki Warm Springs are so close you can have a swim instead of shower. The types of accommodation are as follows:

Super suite
VIP suite   (Recommended)
Special double   (Recommended)
Family Chalet
Old Double

The restaurant is variable, but we were able to get simple but acceptable food for dinner on our last visit. It is advisable to take some of your own food, especially tins, breakfasts cereals and snacks for picnics. There is a small shop in the camp which sells a few items of food, and there is a bar for beer and soft drinks, but these are not always open.

Index

Aba (Abia State), 50-51
Abakaliki, 51
Abeokuta, 11-13
Abraka, 13-14
Abraka River Resort Motel
   See Hotels
Abuja: Federal Capital Territory, 1, 78-79
Abuyazidu, Bayajidda, 87-88
Adire Cloth, 12, 22, 51
   See also Weaving/Weavers
Afikpo-Ishiagu Pottery, 51-52
   See also Pottery
African Timber and Plywood
   Company (AT&P), 47
Agbogun (Son of Olofin), 24
Agbokim Waterfalls, 52
Agho, Mr W A, 18
Agulu Lake, 52
Agura Hotel,
   See Hotels
Ahmadu Bello University, Zaria, 102
AIDS, *xii*
Ayetoro Commune Village, 14-15
Ake, 12-13
Akong, SE
Akwete Cloth, 51
Akwete Textile Centre, 53
   See also Weaving/Weavers
Alaba Market,
   See Markets
Alake of Egbaland (Palace), 12
Alfa Alimi's Mosque and Residence (Ilorin), 30
Alok Stone Monoliths, 53-54
Amina, Queen, 96
Apapa, 2-3
Argungu, 80-82
   — Fishing Festival 80-82
Arochukwu Shrine (The Long Juju), 54-55
Art and Crafts, 4
Artefacts, 4
Aso Oke Cloths, 22

Assop Falls, 114
Assumpta Catholic Cathedral, 70
Azumini Blue River, 72

Baboons, 122, 127
Badagry, 16
Bagauda Lake Hotel,
   See Hotels
Baikie's Boat, 34
Balogun Market,
   See Markets
Bar Beach Market
   See Markets
Batik Materials, 12
Bauchi, 107-108
Beaches, 5-6
Beadmaking, 83
Beatty, Balfour, 35-36
Benin-City, 16-21
   — moat, 18
Benue Hotel
   See Hotels
Bida, 83-84
   — 8-legged Stools, 83
Birds/Bird watching, 65, 84, 93, 109, 120-121, 127.
Birikisu (Woman legend), 25-26
Birnin Gwari, 84-85
Birnin Kebbi, 85
Birnin Kudu, 85
Boat trips (in Rivers State), 71
Bonny, 71
Borno: Kingdom of, 87
Brasswork, 83
British Council Library, *x*
Bronze making, 17, 28, 35
Bulatura Oases, 108-109

Calabar, 55-58
Calabash Workshop, 30
Camels, 99

Cardew, Michael, 101
Carvings, 69-70
Chafe, 86
Clapperton's Tomb, 100-101
Crowther, Bishop Samuel Ajayi, 39

Dada Pottery Workshop, 30
   See also Pottery
Dagona Wildfowl Sanctuary, 121
Dasuki, Alhaji Ibrahim, 100
Daura, 86-88
Davies, Nike, 42
Didi museum,
   See Museums
Dikwa, 109-110
Dogon Ruwa River, 84
Driving licence, *xi*
Daura, 87
Dye - pits, 77, 94

Edo Kingdom, 16-17
Ebohon Cultural Centre, 18-19
Egba (People), 12
Eleko beach, 6
   See also Beaches.
El-Kanemi, 116
Enugu, 58-59
Erin-Ijesa Falls, 21-22
Esie town, 31
Esie Museum, 31
   See, Museums
Ethiope River, 13, 20
Etsu Nupe (the Emir of Nupe), 83
Ezeonwuka, Chief R A, 73

Federal Palace Hotel,
   See Hotels
First-aid kit, *xii*
First Storey House, 16
Frobenius, Leo, 28
Fulani, 42, 100
   — bride-choosing ceremony; 86
   — uprisings, 116
Funfairs: in Lagos, 6-7

Gagi River, 126
Gallery:
   — National, of Modern Art, Craft and
      Design, National Theatre Iganmu, 4
Gardens, 7
Gashaka-Gumti Game Reserve, 59-60

Gateway International Hotel,
   See Hotels
Geidam, 110
Geji Rock Paintings, 107, 110-111
Geologists, 125
Gidan Makama Museum
   See Museums
Goborau Minaret, 96
Golf club/course, 79, 90, 113
Gorgoram, 111
Gurara Falls, 88-89
Gwoza hills, 111

Hadejia-Nguru Wetlands Project, 107, 109, 120
Handicrafts, 8
Hausa/Fulani traditions, 77, 100
   — Kingdom: Legend about origin, 87-88
   See also Fulani
Hippos/hippopotamus, 113, 122
Hotels:
   — Abraka River Resort, 14
   — Agura (Abuja), 79
   — Akure Plaza, 25
   — Bagauda Lake (Kano), 82-83
   — Benue (Markurdi), 61-62
   — Central Hotel (Kano) 95-96
   — Concord Holiday and Health Farm
      Resort (Ilesa), 29-30
   — Country Home (the Ranch-Benin), 19
   — Deribe (Maiduguri), 120
   — Diganga (Ife), 29
   — Durbar and Hamdala (Kaduna), 91
   — Emotan, Benin, 19-20
   — Federal Palace, Lagos, 7-8
   — Gateway International (Abeokuta), 13
   — Grand Fishing, Argungu, 82
   — Guest Inn (Nguru), 121-122
   — Hill Station, Jos, 115
   — Ikoyi Hotel, Lagos, 8
   — Ikwe Holiday Resort, Markurdi, 61
   — Imo Concord, Owerri, 70
   — Kainji Motel, 38
   — Kwara Hotel, 31
   — Lake Chad, Maiduguri, 120
   — L'Hotel Eko Meridien, Lagos, 7
   — Liyafa Palace, (Katsina), 97
   — Metropolitan, Calabar, 57
   — Nicon-Noga Hilton, Abuja, 79-80
   — Nike Lake, Enugu, 58-59
   — Niger Heritage Regency, Onitsha, 69

— Oguta Lake, 71
— Okada Wonderland, Benin, 20
— Osun Presidential, Osogbo, 43
— Owena, Akure, 22, 25
— Palm Grove Motel, 48
— Plateau, 115
— Plaza, Lokoja, 40
— Premier, Ibadan, 23
— Presidential, Port-Harcourt, 72-73
— Rock Castle, Kano, 82
— Sheraton,
  — Abuja, 79
  — Ikeja, Lagos, 7
— The Daula, 63-64
— Tim Tali (Langtang), 125
— Trans-Nigeria Motels, Ibadan, 33-34
— Zaranda, Bauchi, 108

Ibadan, 22-23
Idanre, 23-25
Id-el-Fitri, 77, 88
  See also Sallah Festivals
Id-el-Maulud, 77, 88
  See also Sallah Festivals
Igbeti (town), 31
Igbinakpogie, Mr John, 19
Igbo, 58
Igbo - Ukwu, 60-61
Igue Festival, 17
  See also Festivals
Ijebu-Ode Birikisu-Sungbo Shrine, Oke Eri, 25-26
Ikogosi Warm Springs, 26-27
Ikot-Ekpene, 60
Ikoyi Hotel
  See Hotels
Ile-Ife, 27-30
Ilorin, 30-32
Imo Concord Hotel
  See Hotels
Inselbergs, 77
  — Abuja, 78
  — Ado Awaye, 32
  — Ogboro, 32
Iseyin, 32-34
Insurance: Car, *xii*
International Institute for Tropical Agriculture (IITA), 22
"Iron of Liberty", 39

Jacaranda Restaurant and Pottery (Kaduna), 90
Jakpa, 21, 47
Jankara Market,
  See Markets
Jebba, 34-35
Jihad, 100
Jos, 112-116
Jos Wildlife Park, 112
Juju Rock, 34-35

Kabanci display, 80
Kabawa, 80
Kaduna, *ix*, 89-91
Kafanchan/Kagoro, 91-93
Kagoro Boy Scout Camp, 92-93
Kagoro Forest, 93
Kainji dam,
  See also Lake Kainji National Park, 35-36
Kamberi Villages, 37
Kamuku Wildlife reserve, 84
Kano, 93-96
Kanta, Mohammed, 81-82
Kanuris, 119
Katsina, 96-97
Kazaure, 97-98
Kebbi Empire, 81
Kofar Yandaka, 96
Koko, 20
Koton-Karifi, 97
Kwa Falls, 56-57
Kwali, Dr Ladi, 101
Kwara Hotel
  See Hotels
Kwayatera Waterfall, 118
Kukawa, 116-117
Kurra Falls, 114, 117

Lake Chad, 118
Lake Kainji National Park (Borgu Sector), 35-38
Lagos, 1
Lander, Richard, 100
Leather Work, 77
Lekki Peninsula,
  See Beaches
Liyafa Palace Hotel
  See Hotels
Lokoja, 39-40
Lugard, Lord, 39

Mado Tourist Village, 115
Maiduguri, 119-120
Maiyegun Beach,
   See also Beaches
Markurdi, 61-62
Mambilla Plateau, 62-64
Mandara Mountains, 123
Manor House, 33
Markets:
— Alaba, 3
— Ariara (Aba), 50
— Balogun (Lagos), 2
— Bar Beach, 3
— Fulani (Chafe), 86
— Jajimaji, 121
— Jankara, 2
— Jos Ultra-modern, 113
— Kurmi, 95
— Oba's (Benin), 18
— Oje (Ibadan), 22
— Pottery (Lokoja - Kaduna road), 79
Matan Fada, 80
Mera, Alhaji Muhammadu, 80
Metal Work (Glass) (Bida), 77
Minna, 98-99
Missionaries, 11, 16, 55
Mount Patti, 39-40
Museums:
— of Architecture and Zoo, Jos; 112
— Benin, 17
— Bornu State, 119
— of Colonial History (Aba), 51
— Didi, 4
— Esie, 31
— Gidan Makama, 94
— Ile-Ife, 28
— Mbari (Owerri), 70
— Kanta, 81
— National (Calabar), 56
— National (Onikan, Lagos), 4
— Nsukka Campus, 64
— Oron, 67-70
— Regimental, of the Nigerian Army, 102
— River State, 71
— Umahia National War, 73-74

Naraguta leather works and pottery, 114
NESCO (Bukoro-Jos), 117
Nguru, 120-123
Nicon - Noga Hilton Hotels
   See Hotels
Nigerian Conservation Foundation (NCF), 20
Nigerian Field Society (NFS), 41
Nigerian Tobacco Company (NTC), 32
Niger river, 35
Nike Lake Hotel (Enugu)
   See Hotels
NOK terracotta heads, 4, 112
Nsukka, 64

Obafemi Awolowo University, Ile-Ife, 29
Oban hills, 56-57
Obudu Cattle Ranch, 64-67
Oduduwa, 27
Offa, 40
Ogbunike cave, 67-68
Ogun River, 11
Oguta Lake Resort, 68-69
"Ojukwu Bunker", 68
Okada Wonderland
   See Hotels
Oke-Iho Village, 33
Okomu Forest Reserve, 20
Okuta Ilo Irin (Stone for Sharpening metal tools at Ilorin), 30
Olodumare, 27
Olumo rock, 11-12
Omo Forest, 41
Onimoko Yam Festival, 40
Onitsha, 69
Ooni of Ife's Palace, 28
Opa Oranyan/Oranmiyan, 28
Opobo, 71-72
Ornithologists, 120
Oron, 69-70
   See also Museum
Oshogbo, 42-43
Ososo, 43-44
Oshun shrine (goddess), 42
Owa's palace, 24
Owerri, 70-71
Owo, 44
Owu (Ore) Falls, 44-45

Paintings, 85, 107, 110-111
Pandam Wildlife Park, 122-123
Pankshin, 123
Park, Mungo, 34
Patani, 45-46
Pategi, 46

Peking Chinese Restaurant, 96
Pelican's nest (white), 125
Polo tournament, 90
Port Harcourt (The Garden city), 71-73
Pottery, 12, 77, 90, 112, 123
— Dada's workshop (Ilorin), 30

Railway engine graveyard (Kafanchan), 92
Rhumsiki valley, 123-124
Rima River, 80
Riyom Rock, 114
Rojenny Tourist village, 73
Royal Society for the Protection of Birds
    (RSPB), 120

Sahara desert, 107
Saki town, 33
Sallah festivals, 77, 88
Salt, xii
Sambisa Game Reserve, 124
Sapele, 47
Sarki snake, 87
Shaw, Thurstan, 60
Sheraton Hotels,
    See Hotels
Shere hills, 113
Slave trade, 11, 16
Slessor, Mary, 55-56
Sokoto, 76, 99-101
Soyinka, Wole, 13
Suleja, 101-102
Sultan, of Sokoto, 96, 99-100

Tafawa Balewa's Tomb, 108
Tangale Hill, 124-125
Tarkwa Bay, 5
    See also Beaches
Tinubu Square (Lagos), 2
Tsetse fly, 127
Twin Seven Seven, 42

Umuahia National War Museum
    See Museums
University of Ibadan, (U.I.), 22
Usman, dan Fodio, 100
Usuma dam and reservoir (Abuja), 78
Uwuru Rapids, 37
Vong Nfwei Hill, 113

Wallace, Mr PT, 125
Warri, 48

Wase Rock/hill (Jos), 115, 125
Weaving/Weavers, 32
Wenger, Suzanne, 42-43
West Africa, xiv
Whispering Palms, 6
Wikki Warm Springs, 126-128
Wood Carving, 18
Wurno, 102

Yankari Game Reserve, 126-129
Yola, 74-75
Yorubaland, 22

Zaria, 102-103
Zoo, 22, 95, 112
Zuma rock, 77, 103
Zungeru, 104